EVERY PERFECT
Possibility

A STORY OF
HOPE AND SURRENDER

LISA DRIBNENKI
WITH BRIAN DRIBNENKI

EVERY PERFECT POSSIBILITY
Copyright © 2024 by Lisa Dribnenki

All rights reserved. Neither this publication nor any part of this publication may be reproduced or transmitted in any form or by any means, electronic or mechanical, including photocopying, recording or any information storage and retrieval system, without permission in writing from the author.

Scripture quotations marked ASV are taken from the Holy Bible, American Standard Version, which is in the public domain. • Scripture quotations marked ESV are from The Holy Bible, English Standard Version® (ESV®), copyright ©2001 by Crossway, a publishing ministry of Good News Publishers. Used by permission. All rights reserved • Scripture quotations marked NIV are taken from the Holy Bible, NEW INTERNATIONAL VERSION®, NIV® Copyright © 1973, 1978, 1984, 2011 by Biblica, Inc.® Used by permission. All rights reserved worldwide. • Scripture quotations marked AMP taken from the Amplified® Bible, Copyright © 1954, 1958,1962, 1964, 1965, 1987 by The Lockman Foundation. Used by permission. • Scripture quotations marked NKJV taken from the New King James Version®. Copyright © 1982 by Thomas Nelson, Inc. Used by permission. All rights reserved.

This book is a memoir and is based on true events. It reflects the author's present recollections of personal experiences over time. The information contained in this book is by no means a substitute for the advice of a qualified medical professional. In order to maintain the privacy as well as the anonymity of certain individuals involved in this story, names have been changed to protect their privacy.

Soft Cover ISBN: 978-1-4866-2606-9
Hard Cover ISBN: 978-1-4866-2613-7
ebook ISBN: 978-1-4866-2612-0

Word Alive Press
119 De Baets Street Winnipeg, MB R2J 3R9
www.wordalivepress.ca

Cataloguing in Publication information can be obtained from Library and Archives Canada.

DEDICATED TO:
Brian, my knight in shining armour,
my love, my best friend.
Our sons,
Derek, my friendly, social one
Scott, my cuddly, happy one
Travis, my baby, the gentle one.
Our loving family and friends
who have walked this journey with us.
And God Almighty,
who has blessed us with this healing gift.

Contents

Foreword	vii
Introduction	xi
One: **Diagnosis**	1
Two: **God, Not Google**	7
Three: **Scans, Scans, and More Scans**	13
Four: **Remove the Fluffy Stuff**	21
Five: **I'm Not Afraid Anymore**	27
Six: **Of Geese and Angels**	35
Seven: **Find Hope, Keep Hope, Build Hope**	47
Eight: **Scans, Scans, and More Tumours!!**	59

Nine: **Passing Time**	63
Ten: **God Can Do the Impossible**	71
Eleven: **Chemo Has Come**	77
Twelve: **A Complicated Mess**	87
Thirteen: **North to Alaska**	93
Fourteen: **Stable is a Big Word**	101
Fifteen: **Testing... Testing...**	107
Sixteen: **Healed**	113
About the Author	137
Further Reading	139
Endnotes	141

Foreword

JUST BECAUSE YOU can't see the sun on a cloudy day, doesn't mean the sun isn't there.

Shortly after Brian and Lisa shared their devastating news with my husband Bill and me—on the evening I will never forget—I came across the above phrase. It was exactly what I needed to hear at that time. Thank you, God.

The sun of course represents a divine spiritual force. As a friend of theirs, I needed a strong reminder that when I am feeling powerless to help, there is a power in this universe that is much greater than me. A power you can draw strength and comfort from. I had to believe that Brian and Lisa were going to be okay. I leaned on my faith. *Please, God, help them get through this.*

We first met Brian and Lisa in 2012, shortly after we moved right next door to them. The four of us soon developed a beautiful friendship and discovered we shared many similar interests. We just clicked. We hit the jackpot with our new neighbours! Often, I would consciously appreciate how well we connected with each other and felt strongly that God had led us to live exactly where we were. I have come to believe that none of the people you meet in life cross your path by accident. Each encounter is meant for a reason. I am so thankful Brian and Lisa are part of our lives, and I believe we're here to share part of their journey, particularly the events of the last few years.

Lisa writes a lot about miracles in this beautiful memoir. She points out that miracles are everywhere; you just have to take the time to notice them. A miracle can be as little or as big as a change in perspective. For example, the way you choose to see things. Lisa and Brian have chosen to face this health battle with hope and optimism. They choose faith over fear. This in itself is a miracle! It is truly amazing to watch them work as a team as they take on this battle! What an incredible example of love.

As you read this memoir, I think you'll feel the love coming from Lisa's words—straight from her heart, throughout the whole book. She's an incredibly honest woman with a beautiful heart. I believe she is a true messenger, sent to speak of faith, love, and hope. She openly describes finding her purpose, overcoming the trials of getting there, and ultimately does a beautiful job of sharing how she and Brian took steps together to find hope, keep hope, and build hope.

FOREWORD

This book has many dimensions. It's about a journey through cancer diagnosis and treatment. It's about moving from absolute despair to surrender— surrender to a greater source, a greater power. To God. It's about the importance of family and community. It is about creating an experience that allows you to live in tremendous gratitude and appreciation for everything around you while, at the same time, taking on the greatest challenge of your lives. It's a love story.

Thank you, my dear friend Lisa, for the opportunity to be part of your journey. I am truly honoured to contribute in some small way to this gift you're sharing with the world. I wholeheartedly admire your grace, strength, courage, love, and devotion. Thank you for opening your heart and this very private part of your lives for the greater good of helping others. I love you too.

—Brenda

Introduction

"BRIAN, YOU HAVE cancer."

I will never forget these words or the emotion they created. How could I? We were talking about *cancer*. The big C! Everything about that day will remain transfixed in my mind: the weather; the phone call we received on the way home from Edmonton, Alberta; even the road where we pulled over to take the doctor's call. Literally everything changed in that moment. I still get chills when we drive by the spot where we took the dreadful call on that beautiful winter day. February 16, 2021.

This book is my attempt to tell *our* story. It's a very personal journey, from the deepest moments of despair to complete surrender. This book is not just another cancer story but a story of faith, hope, and love. Despite the fact that Brian has cancer, I refer to everything happening to us as a couple. *We* had a test, *we* had scans, or *we* just had a great doctor's appointment. I was committed to this journey— that *we* would take it together, battle it together, and with hope, *we* would defeat it together!

Whether you are a patient, survivor, loved one, widow, friend, or colleague, cancer will change you forever. Though we try to convince others that we're the same, we simply won't be. For our family, cancer would transform everything about our lives.

Don't rush to conclusions. Cancer has brought some of our most powerful and spiritual blessings—a time of gratitude and peace that's become the centre of our faithful journey. Despite our circumstances, I am certain that *we* will rise up, better and stronger. Closer to God and even closer to each other.

What happened during our journey and in our most difficult circumstances? Renewed faith in the Almighty and a message so powerful that I had no choice but to speak of its greatness and completely surrender to its care.

The title *Every Perfect Possibility* is our way of turning a cancer death sentence into something more: a time of hope and gratitude that drew us together and delivered a peace beyond understanding. My prayer is that, through our experience, you too will find comfort as well as a renewed spiritual awareness. There is a higher power, and we have all come from the almighty one. We are on this journey together—and together, we find God!

INTRODUCTION

And now these three remain: faith, hope, and love. But the greatest of these is love. (1 Corinthians 13:13, NIV)

One
Diagnosis

FOLLOWING THE DREADED call on the side of Highway 28, we began a long and emotional medical journey. Our first appointment was at the Cross Cancer Institute—CCI, which sounds like an undercover special ops force. We truly were special forces, operating under God's force. At this point, the number of people praying for us was certainly equal to a special forces squadron. It had been a few weeks since Brian was diagnosed with lung cancer, and following a CT scan, PET scan, and biopsy, we finally received the specifics on the staging and type of cancer he had.

Being thrown into the world of cancer—and walking into a hospital like the CCI—is a real kick in the butt. The whole ordeal feels strange and scary. Wonderful, caring faces do their best to greet you with a smile and drag your sorry self wherever you need to go. Cancer survivors and volunteers don burgundy vests and quickly recognize the lost and anxious faces who need a kind soul to guide them through the halls. All around, patients of various ages and backgrounds wear the same apprehensive look. Cancer patients have a deep connection to each other; it's called survival! As we have discovered on this journey, not only did our faith grow, but the connection to people within our cancer and support community grew as well. These experiences and emotions elevated us on our journey.

Looking around Waiting Room 1, we couldn't help but feel out of place. The old Sesame Street song "One of These Things is Not Like the Other" came to mind. Brian was so much younger and healthier looking than the other patients we saw there. He seemed *stronger*. It really felt like we'd taken the wrong bus. We'd planned to tape our appointment—something recommended by others who'd endured this same crazy experience. Taping the appointment is necessary because your brain is not ready to deal with everything that's going on. At that point, we were just trying to process the diagnosis. Following a brief introduction, our oncologist picked up his black marker and began charting our new reality on his whiteboard. I guess in cancer, things are just that black-and-white. We had entered the Twilight Zone, a state of mind between fantasy and reality. I was numb.

Non-small cell lung cancer. Adenocarcinoma, EGFR Exon 19 Deletion. He referred to this as a mutation. The primary tumour was in the left lung, but the cancer had already spread to several areas in the

ONE: DIAGNOSIS

bone. The doctor asked about his symptoms and about shortness of breath. About bone pain. Brian told him he'd worked as a tradesman for years and had assumed most of his pain was the result of physically demanding work—just normal aches and discomfort. I was in denial. I didn't want to believe what I was being told. It was one thing to hear that Brian had lung cancer and another to hear it had already moved to his bones. "Are you sure it's not arthritis?" I asked. They say there are no stupid questions, right? At that moment, the doctor gave me a look that said, *That was a stupid question!* In my mind, I was rehearsing all the cases I'd read about, cases of misread PET scans and errors in interpreting medical exams. This had to be one of those mistakes. It just didn't make sense. Yes, we had a biopsy, and the tumour had been identified, but other than his annoying cough and some weight loss, Brian looked strong and healthy.

Brian has always struggled with lung capacity and, for a never-smoker, had always had poor results on his annual health and safety assessments. We'd always thought, *Everyone is different, right? Not all of us have the same lung capacity, and not all of us will be marathon runners.* But now, we were learning so much more about what had likely been going on for years! The doctor was quite certain this cancer had been progressing for some time now. Many times, Brian went to the doctor and was told he was a young, healthy nonsmoker. The fact that Brian did not smoke was actually a detriment to accessing some of the screening that should have been done to better assess his cough.

We were shocked as he went on to tell us that this mutation mainly affects young, female, Asian non-smokers. Hmmm, another Sesame Street moment! Our oncologist continued to explain that Brian was stage four. *Terminal*. There was no way to eliminate the cancer, but their treatment goals aimed to improve his quality and quantity of life. Just like that, from zero to sixty, Brian sped past all the other checkpoints and was going for the gusto. I'm certainly not poking fun at him or our situation, but why couldn't he have travelled this path more gradually, to give us time to adjust to the reality? The doc drew a bell curve. The dreaded marking system. That day we received a poor grade, the average being thirty-six to thirty-nine months of life. And that's cancer. The brutal reality of a disease known far too well by far too many. Brian's family has certainly come to know it well. For generations, many relatives on his maternal side have faced the same terrible disease at a very young age. With the exception of Brian's mother, all of them have lost their lives to cancer early in life.

The good news about all this, the oncologist told us, was that Brian could be treated by a targeted therapy drug (TKI) called osimertinib. We began to refer to it as Ozzy. Unlike chemotherapy, TKI incredibly targets only the cancer cells, stabilizing the disease and inhibiting cancer growth. There was hope. This gave us some time to work with. I was still processing all this, along with the thought, But what about the man? This doctor didn't know my husband. You won't find a more committed, determined, strong man anywhere. If he could approach this disease the way he always approached life—if anyone could beat this—it would be Brian! At the end of our initial appointment, I told the doctor we planned to blow those numbers and averages out of the water!

What came next was the most distressing part of it all: telling our family and friends what we had just learned. We dreaded telling Travis, our youngest son. Just fifteen years old, he was at such a vulnerable time of his life. I began to wonder about each of them. How would Derek cope? He lived so far from home over there in Ireland as he completed his third year of dental school. This was going to add even more stress to his already demanding workload. I also worried about Scott. He was the most like Brian of all our boys. Thankfully, he had Brianna in his life to support him. It pained me to think how each of them would manage without such an amazing, supportive dad in their lives.

Stop. I couldn't let this disease destroy our family. I remembered to shift—positive thoughts only! I was too programmed to think of the negative thoughts first, letting my mind go to crazy, scary places. Starting immediately, I needed to change my thought pattern in order to save my sanity and improve how I'd handle all this. Sometimes that's easier said than done!

We had lots of time to think on the way home about what was happening and what it meant for us. My mind kept crashing. Terrible negative thoughts prevailed, and I was focused on the cancer, worrying about how quickly it might defeat him. Words like *terminal, palliative,* and *end of life planning* had entered our vocabulary that day. I knew this wasn't the way to handle this situation. The battle of the minds began. The ego vs. the Holy Spirit. Fear vs. faith. Our healing journey had truly begun.

Our Greatest Gifts.
Brian and sons Scott, Derek, and Travis, 2020.

Two
God, Not Google

SOON AFTER BRIAN'S diagnosis, I began a frenzy of research. Sitting at the computer every day, talking to people on the phone, reading blogs and books, searching clinical trials, calling advocates like Lung Cancer Canada—even ordering a radon meter for the house. According to the Canadian Cancer Society, Health Canada estimates about sixteen percent of lung cancer deaths are related to radon exposure in the home. Radon exposure is the leading cause of lung cancer in nonsmokers, and it's estimated that in Canada there are more than 3 300 lung cancer deaths related to radon each year. It's crazy how quickly the information consumed me and ate away our precious time together. I wondered, Is this all worthwhile or simply a distraction?

I found three different social media groups through Facebook: Tagrisso Patients & Caregivers, EGFR Resistors, and Matt's Alive. I even stumbled across two other cases in our home province of Alberta. One of these was Matt, a young father in his late thirties; the other was a young mother named Kelsey, diagnosed while expecting her second child. She also was in her thirties.

Kelsey's story appeared in the local news and was so like Brian's. Complaints of a nagging cough. Several appointments. Doctors not listening to concerns about a persistent cough. Prescriptions for other medications, including asthma puffers. The message: "You don't smoke. You're young and healthy." Basically, they ruled out cancer without proper screening. Not even so much as an X-ray. The truth is anyone with lungs can get lung cancer. If I could broadcast anything loud and clear, I'd want people to know this: be diligent, and do not let doctors tell you that you're too young or healthy! So many cases of this type of lung cancer are exactly those people—young, strong, and healthy athletes, mothers, fathers, sons, and daughters. Just like Brian, Matt, and Kelsey.

I saw that many members in our social media groups were younger than Brian. I also noticed that others from around the world did not have basic insurance coverage to pay for the cost of this drug, Ozzy. Now was not the time to wallow in self-pity and sadness. Thank God! I realized we had so much to be grateful for when I considered all these other situations.

I am an information seeker. I needed some answers, but honestly, some of this stuff was way over

TWO: GOD, NOT GOOGLE

my head! We connected with a company from Vancouver who would help us better understand things and do regular blood tests measuring the amount of EGFR protein in Brian's blood. We were told they could determine, through regular blood work, if the treatment was working even before scans revealed changes. This was one of the first things we decided to do. After consulting, they also asked us to send a tumour sample to a company in France who would provide more information about potential biomarkers not typically assessed in tumour biopsies. Thinking this might answer some questions about the cancer in Brian's family, we agreed to have the test done. The cost for this was quite extensive, but worthwhile; and we had family who offered to help with the expense. We set a budget of fifteen thousand dollars and hoped we could get more information to help Brian fight this cancer and stay ahead of it. Is it possible to stay ahead of cancer? How can you even set a budget on saving your loved one? We knew that, whatever it took, we would find a way to help Brian *battle* this disease.

All cancer cells have mutations, abnormal molecular changes that allow them to grow and divide uncontrollably. Although smoking causes most lung cancers, we now know there are also many people like Brian who have never smoked, yet still develop the deadliest cancer out there—lung cancer. Today, public awareness is growing. Several new targeted therapies and trials are in the works to treat this type of lung cancer, a disease that affects so many young nonsmokers. It all seems very promising and hopeful. We are grateful for Ozzy, which became available in Canada in 2018, and thankful that this lifesaving drug was covered by healthcare at a whopping cost of ten thousand dollars a month!

We would later enlist the help of the Dana-Farber Hospital in Boston. There, a specialized team of twelve doctors worked at the Chen-Huang Center for EGFR-Mutant Lung Cancers, advancing patient care through their research and clinical trials. Dr. Maillot became our virtual doctor. We were grateful to have another expert opinion, readily available via Zoom consultation and at a cost of twelve hundred dollars per appointment. His knowledge and expertise would support our oncologist as new situations arose with Brian's care and treatment plan.

A word of caution: Google can consume you and is not always helpful when dealing with this type of diagnosis. I'm sure we all know this, having researched many of our own fatal, false diagnoses through Dr. Google. Knowledge is power, but it's also a plague when it comes to this type of circumstance. It leads you to believe your situation is no different than any other. You're going to die of cancer regardless of what you do, who you know, or how you battle this dreadful disease. If Steve Jobs, with all his money, couldn't stop the cancer beast, how will we?

TWO: GOD, NOT GOOGLE

In Smoky Lake, Alberta, returning from an appointment in Edmonton, I made a stop and peered to my left. The sign at a small church on the street said, "Turn to God, not Google!" A clear-cut message from the big guy himself. We were not in control of this situation, no matter how much effort and research I put into the topic. The matter was truly in God's hands. With an outlook that anticipated *every perfect possibility*, we would defy the odds. EPPIC— Every Perfect Possibility In Christ. Brian would receive a healing miracle!

Three
Scans, Scans, and More Scans

ALTHOUGH I AM intent on writing a book that's not just about cancer, I feel it is necessary to provide some context to our cancer journey. Scans happened every three months from the point of diagnosis. Initially, we had very pleasing results with Ozzy. Like many others on this TKI, the tumours were responding well to the drug. Evidence through his scans showed the tumour in the left lung had shrunk, and cancerous areas of bone were no longer evident or had also shrunk in size. Amazing, right? Most people with cancer will never experience this kind of result. Tumours shrinking and even disappearing. Poof—like magic, Ozzy was doing its job. The targeted therapy drug attacked the cancer cells and eliminated them.

Scan days were physically hard on him, whether it was an IV or CTs on the chest and abdomen, full body, and bones. Initially, a PET scan was used to diagnose him, but we soon discovered that no one had looked at the brain. We were told by our company in Vancouver that with stage four lung cancer, the new protocol was to do a brain scan. We learned that lung cancer has a common metastatic pattern: lung-bone-brain or lung-brain-bone.

It was now September. We were seven months into our cancer journey. One of our new adventures was a trip to Harrison Hot Springs in British Columbia to celebrate Brian's fiftieth birthday. Everything was stable now, and the meds were working, so why not? We wanted to make the most of every possible opportunity while Brian was feeling well.

On his birthday, he told me, "Well, at least I made my fiftieth. My grandfather, uncle, and cousin never had a chance to celebrate their fiftieth birthdays!" My heart sank. How very sad and true. This disease had stolen so much from his family—and from so many others. Why had this family already endured so much pain from cancer? Was there anything we could do to change this? *Lord, I ask you to guide us in our healing journey and lead us toward you.*

Meditative Prayer (St. Francis of Assisi)
Lord, make me an instrument of your peace:
where there is hatred, let me sow love;
where there is injury, pardon;
where there is doubt, faith;
where there is despair, hope;
where there is darkness, light;

THREE: SCANS, SCANS AND MORE SCANS

where there is sadness, joy.
O divine Master, grant that I may not so much seek
to be consoled as to console,
to be understood as to understand,
to be loved as to love;
For it is in giving that we receive;
it is in pardoning that we are pardoned;
it is in dying that we are born to eternal life.
Amen (I Believe)

The birthday trip was going great in this pretty little town with tons of character and touristy charm. We hit the jackpot by finding the Black Forest Restaurant, the best German restaurant ever! There were several other amazing little spots, including a beach area filled with excitement, joy, and laughter. Later in our trip, Brian and I rented a bicycle-built-for-two to cruise the streets. It looked like fun, and everyone was doing it. Why not?

Not at all comfortable on this odd side-by-side bicycle, we both found the pedals awkward and difficult to reach. Stretching to reach and maneuver the bike, we managed an hour along the quaint streets of Harrison. We took some pictures to add to the *memory* bank, the most precious and valuable bank of all. That night it happened: strange electric shocks started running through Brian's right leg. I immediately told myself it was that darn bicycle ride and the strange position we were peddling from. I confidently stated,

"Brian, you must have pinched a nerve." We agreed, and Brian laughed it off, saying, "It would have helped if you had contributed a little more effort to our bike ride!"

Back home, the shocks continued, progressing to a point where Brian's leg had a complete seizure. It was bouncing uncontrollably while helping Scott inside his boat. Again, it always seemed to happen when he was in an awkward position. The doctor assessed him in the clinic and, convinced it is severe sciatica, suggested chiropractic, acupuncture, and physiotherapy. The first time he went to see the physiotherapist, his leg had a seizure while she was in the room. She had never seen anything like this, and it threw her into a panic.

After several episodes of weakness, muscle tightening, seizures, and cramping, we decided to visit the local emergency room. Brian explained the situation very well, including the fact that it all started after the dreaded bike ride. Is there a connection to the bike, or is it just coincidence? We overheard the doctor's phone conversation with an on-call physician at the Cross Cancer Institute. Quickly, an emergency appointment was ordered at the Cross, and we headed into the city later that week.

We proceeded to the radiology department and met with the radiologist. Dr. Gyner had been caring for cancer patients for decades—this guy knew his stuff! Feeling unsure about it all, we wondered why we were even in the radiology area. Once again, Brian

THREE: SCANS, SCANS AND MORE SCANS

explained the symptoms and what was happening in his leg. He was asked about headaches. None. Dizziness? None. Weakness? None. It was just the bike; honestly, we believed we were dealing with a pinched nerve and just wanted someone to fix it! After consulting, he ordered a quick brain MRI and told us it may be a very deadly condition called Leptomeningeal Disease (LMD). Now I was sick with fear.

Following the brain MRI, the doctor returned to say, "Brian, it's a single brain tumour." I was now numb. The tumour was on the left side parietal lobe. It might explain the problem with his leg, but it might not. This was still questionable. Brian would need brain radiation. Ozzy was supposed to take care of this kind of stuff. It can cross the blood-brain barrier, so why was this happening? Had the tumour always been there, and they'd missed it? No one had really looked at his brain initially. I began to wonder, Is it a new mutation? The doctor had spoken about how smart cancer is and how quickly it will change. Was this something new that the medication was not addressing anymore? Regardless, we had to trust that God had brought us to the discovery of the tumour and to hope and healing for Brian.

Within a week, he was fitted with a radiation helmet and booked for single brain radiation on the tumour. *It's just another setback*, I thought. Maybe God knew the tumour was there for a long time and needed to be dealt with. Maybe that crazy bike ride was just a coincidence and helped us find this brain tumour? I still didn't believe the leg was connected to the tumour, but all the doctors told us it was. Whose reports would I listen to—the doctors' or God's? Such a puzzling situation. One of many we would encounter, leaving us all without answers but forcing us to trust in God's divine guidance.

Bicycle-built-for-two. Harrison, B.C., 2021

THREE: SCANS, SCANS AND MORE SCANS

Brian's 50th birthday. Harrison Lake, B.C., 2021

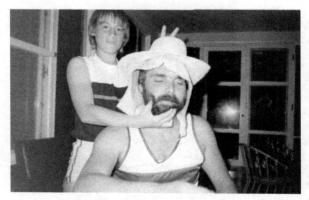

Brian and his special Uncle Jurgen. Cuba, 1984

Four
Remove the Fluffy Stuff

LIFE IS BUSY. Life consumes us, and we can get lost in a sea of things to do, places to go, and work to accomplish. Top that off with a barrage of social media, emails, and news, and the day passes without truly experiencing it. When we received Brian's diagnosis, I made an intentional decision to be more present. We had all heard about mindfulness and living in the moment, but for me, it was baby steps. Daily reminders to mentally, emotionally, and physically put away all the fluffy stuff and just experience the "now" moments.

What does it really mean to be present? It means stretching and feeling your body release tension. Hearing the birds when you wake up in the morning. Noticing the clouds in the sky and oddly realizing what they remind you of. Connecting with nature and feeling the earth under your feet. Smelling the fresh air and feeling the sun's warmth on your body. Watching snowflakes fall on your face. Patiently waiting for the birds to sit at the feeder and enjoying the moment the hummingbird actually sits still while it feeds. Yes, their wings actually do stop moving! Observing children at play or your dog trying to catch that pesky fly. It is truly trying to remove the noise and share each and every moment with the deepest appreciation and gratitude for the gift of life and God's blessings. Pause, notice, and appreciate the miracles all around you.

I recall one special day following Brian's diagnosis. I went out in the fresh snow with our beloved Hercules, our family dog. I somehow felt like a child again, full of joy and freedom. How was it possible—with everything we were dealing with—to feel so at peace and happy? This is truly not my normal state of mind. My mind is normally full of what I need to do today: tasks, lists, errands. I cannot explain it, but in that moment, there was complete peace of mind and joy in my heart. Some may refer to it as a Holy Instant. Whatever it was, it was euphoric! No drugs, just a deep and captivating calm. Living in the moment. Present. I have since read that we all feel time passing so quickly, but it is because we are not really present. The more we feel things slipping by quickly, the less present we are. We lose track of time as we are not truly experiencing it. The question we must ask ourselves is not "Where has the time gone?" but "Where have I been?"

In the fresh snow, I traced out a large heart and listened intently to the sound the birds were making. We were so fortunate to be surrounded by nature.

FOUR: REMOVE THE FLUFFY STUFF

Hope, hope, hope. I heard this aloud from the birds. Since that day, I've listened and watched for the birds, and they continue to make a deep impression on me. It was as if God conveyed a message of hope and strength through the birds. I know it may seem strange to you, but it's like the window to your soul can be opened wide, and suddenly the most amazing experiences, sights, and sounds are within your reach. If you listen, the Holy Spirit is yearning to bring you these gifts, to bring you your true essence. Your heart will speak and bring gifts from the divine that truly touch your soul. Brian and I have encountered many opportunities to feel this peace in the presence of nature and during our prayer time. The birds are now a medium for us to experience the presence of God working in and around us.

This cancer diagnosis has taught us so much about the power of love and connection. We are too easily consumed by objects and material wealth. When we truly experience peace, it awakens our spirit, a place deep within us that connects us to the universe. We realize the power and energy we have will not only provide for us but will deliver us from a place that does not serve us. God knows our true spirit. We are a part of him, and he is in us. As we discover this relationship, we learn that this journey has given us an experience beyond measure. Regardless of your religious belief or nonbelief, this source is working to make you the best you can be.

We always think of the brain as the centre of our being—our central processing unit—but I believe that the heart is at the centre of our life force. It is our true spirit. It is the calling of every human soul to connect with this beautiful source, and this happens in our heart. The capacity lies within us to open and experience this connection, and it comes from the heart, the centre of our being. So many of the answers we're searching for lie within the heart, and sometimes we just need to open up and listen.

If not for our cancer journey, I don't believe we would have experienced these gifts. As difficult as it is to understand, cancer has given us blessings; it has shown us so many things that cannot be explained outside of our journey with God. We chose to trust our future to God and hope in him at all times.

> Trust in the Lord with all your heart, and lean not on your own understanding. In all your ways acknowledge him, and he shall direct your paths. (Proverbs 3:5-6, NKJV)

FOUR: REMOVE THE FLUFFY STUFF

"Man's best friend." Brian and Hercules, 2021.]

Five
I'm Not Afraid Anymore

MANY PARTS OF life are more challenging now, but others are so much better. My whole life, I had been overwhelmed by fear and worry. Mark Twain hit the nail on the head when he said, "I've had a lot of worries in my life, most of which never happened."[1] Countless hours of sleep lost, preoccupation with the "what ifs," negative thoughts, and worry. Fear paralyzed many of my decisions and ruined many experiences as I felt trapped and did not fully embrace them. Looking back, I was always this way. Even as a child, I missed out on so many things as my anxiety took control of nearly every situation. Fear consumed me.

During our most vulnerable time, I hit a point where I was freed from my fear. A huge weight was lifted off me. I felt like Macaulay Culkin in the movie *Home Alone*: "I'm not afraid anymore, I'm *not* afraid anymore!" It was an awakening in the midst of the most painful of circumstances.

A very wise and wonderful friend had told me a couple years before that I had to surrender to God—that I was not in control. It's difficult for me to not control everything or to feel like I'm out of control. I know so many of us understand this. Possibly it's the Type A personality—the perfectionist or overachiever—that might have something to do with the control factor? The moment I decided that I would "give it to God," fear no longer haunted me. What a gift, to be free of fear and trusting God's plan. In the middle of this illness, we learned to accept both joy and sadness at the same time, knowing that we were still going to be okay. Knowing still to trust God's plan. God's got ya!

As we maneuvered through the cancer stuff, I always felt like he had us. A calm and a peace maintained me, and I recall a phone call from Derek in Ireland where I said without hesitation, "I'm going to heal your dad." I spoke so confidently; who did I think I was? It's so strange, but there were many times I felt that confident about Brian's healing. At times, I would reflect on this confidence, saying, Is it real or am I in denial? Regardless, I stuck with the idea that God was directing us down a path to his healing.

One of the times that I believe God was giving me a kick in the pants came on my way to see Mom at the lodge in Vilna. I had developed quite an interest in listening to morning prayers and podcasts. If I was too busy, I would catch up while I was on the road. While traveling on Highway 36, I was deep in

FIVE: I'M NOT AFRAID ANYMORE

thought. Maybe I should have been more observant, but honestly, it was the strangest thing. A big black bear was barrelling out of the ditch right at me. How did I not even see it approaching? It's like it came out of nowhere! Judging by my speed and his location, there was no way I was going to miss him. I'd heard that hitting a bear was like hitting a pig: a large, solid object that was very destructive! Instead of braking, which would have been more logical, someone told me to gun it! I hit the gas hard. That's one thing our Nissan could do—go! There was a vehicle behind me in the distance. It played out in slow motion; honestly, I would love to see it on camera. This big black bear was coming right at me. I literally looked into his eyes and moved my vehicle as far to the shoulder as possible while holding the gas pedal to the floor. He grazed the rear panel on the driver's side, colliding with my tire and rim. I then looked into the rearview mirror as he rolled into the ditch, then ran into the shrubs. *Surreal.*

Safe, I pulled over and inspected the vehicle. It was fine except for some broken plastic and paint that scraped off. I tried to reach Brian at work. I was actually excited about the bear encounter! It's like it gave me this elated feeling. Then I called Scott. "You won't believe what just happened to me. A bear hit me!" I would never admit that I hit the bear, but rather, the bear hit me! At no time was I ever afraid, and I felt totally in control and safe. Every time I pass that spot on the highway, I still wonder what that was all about.

This is my take on that strange situation. God needed to get my attention. He really wanted me to open my eyes and wake up. That is exactly how the encounter with the bear felt. It was a kick in the pants from God. A message of strength. Not only telling me to pay attention, but I think I was also being told I needed to let him take the wheel. I was not in control of this situation, and I had to trust him and let him guide us. Months before, while we were in Harrison, we went into a small gift shop. I bought a necklace with a bear on it. We found out that this was Brian's birth animal for September. Of course, the bear symbolizes courage.

Despite this newfound freedom from fear, it does not mean I am without doubt. I prayed God would help me ignore doubt, fear, and logic. By trusting in him, I know I'm going to be alright, and he has given me the strength to handle this. I choose to live in love, and not let fear destroy me. The one thing I know about fear is that it robs you of your joy. I had become so saturated with fear that it had taken over every part of my life. Even in the midst of moments I should have enjoyed, I was always worrying about something. Our cancer journey has changed that, and I will never live in that place again!

Brian needed to change his attitude toward dealing with fear. He had always been the levelheaded

FIVE: I'M NOT AFRAID ANYMORE

one, telling me not to overreact, not to jump to conclusions. To relax. He was the one who could sleep through the night when Scott was out all night or while Derek was in Ireland during the pandemic. Brian was, without a doubt, always our "protector." Soon after his diagnosis, I took pictures of him teaching the boys different things he felt they needed to know. Travis, how to drive and shave; Scott, how to handle his money; Derek, how to change front wheel bearings and brakes. He's a real champ, always putting us first and planning ahead to make sure that, regardless of the outcome, he will have done everything in his power to take care of us.

Is there anything wrong with being this way, with always being the protector? Being a protector is not a bad thing, unless it also consumes you. He was always planning ahead to avoid every possible mishap or problem. Now, he needed to focus on himself and his healing. He needed to stop trying to fix everything for everyone and let us take care of him. It was very difficult for Brian to ask for help or not be able to do things on his own. As his health changed, he needed to accept this. This is one of the lessons we all need to learn. Sometimes we have to ask for and receive help. That's okay, if we are going to "Wake Up, Heal Up, and Open Up," as Roger Teel says through his brilliant use of acronyms. This one, WHO, speaks of finding and knowing our true selves. Living more powerfully and lovingly while freeing ourselves from those misconceptions and attitudes that do not serve us.

I delved into one of my first books by Bruce H. Lipton, *The Biology of Belief*. The book shed new light onto my understanding of our cells and the balance between growth and protection mode. Dr. Lipton has pushed the boundaries of the scientific understanding of genetics and cell biology. His study of cells creates a new understanding for mind and body connection. This is one area I felt Brian needed to embrace. Always a protector, it was now his time to invest energy in himself and heal what might be impacting his own health. Dr. Lipton's research shows that cells cannot operate efficiently in both growth and protection mode simultaneously; it is necessary to find a balance of these two for the body to thrive. Here is an excerpt from his book that I found very interesting:

> Humans unavoidably restrict their growth behaviors when they shift into a protective mode. Redistributing energy reserves to fuel the protection response inevitably results in a curtailment of growth.[2]

I don't want to target Brian and say that he is not a joyful, loving person. He truly is and has been such a strong, loving father; however, his life had always been

FIVE: I'M NOT AFRAID ANYMORE

centred around protection. Now, he needed to embrace life and just live it without the fear of constantly protecting all he held dear to him, his family.

> When I am afraid, I put my trust in you. In God, whose word I praise—in God I trust and am not afraid. (Psalm 56:3-4, NIV)

Six
Of Geese and Angels

OUR FIRST TRIP to Canmore after Brian's diagnosis, in April 2021, was a difficult one. We had decided to return to celebrate my birthday. Canmore was such a special spot for us. Many family trips, hikes, and adventures had happened in and around the beautiful Alberta Rocky Mountains. Brian always made a point of saying, "Everyone thinks Banff and Jasper are in B.C. Well, guess what? They aren't! Not all of Alberta is dirty oil country!" We need to be more vocal that these beautiful tourist destinations are, in fact, in Alberta. Maybe then people won't think we're such a dirty oil province because they'll all want to come here to enjoy the beautiful landscape, fresh air, and wildlife! Alberta is an amazing province with so much to offer, but it always gets a bad rap. Like cancer, it's just not fair. You can be a kind, loving, hardworking, nonsmoking guy and still get a bad deal. That's Alberta—always getting a bad deal!

EVERY PERFECT POSSIBILITY

This trip felt so different, heavy, and sad. We still looked the same, but inside there was so much sadness, and my chest felt heavy. I wondered if this might be our last trip here. I had been so fortunate that Brian always loved to travel and explore. Together, we had been on many wonderful adventures. He'd exposed our boys to so much knowledge, even if they weren't always interested! Brian would go out of his way to stop and read every information sign and scientific detail. That's one thing that many people wouldn't realize about this quiet guy—the amount of knowledge he has stored up on so many topics. There are plenty of big talkers out there, but sometimes it's the quiet ones that really hold the most truth and understanding. We had always valued the chance to take the boys on vacation and make those memories. Thankfully, I had pictures from many great family vacations. It was different to travel without them now and more difficult to not have their distraction during this trip.

As a child, Brian did a lot of travelling with his parents, but I was lucky to get off the farm and enjoy a few days camping at Fork Lake. If anyone should have had lung cancer, it was me! We would laugh about how Mom would prepare our little old camper before bed with a can of Raid to make sure none of those pesky black flies would bother us early in the morning. I had a great childhood, but our experiences were quite different. Brian truly made my life so incredible. My mom would always tease about how he treated

SIX: OF GEESE AND ANGELS

me like a princess. The Polish Princess! I appreciate all the insight and knowledge Brian always brings to an experience. He is so much more adventurous, and I'm thankful that our sons have that same sense of adventure and thirst for knowledge.

Geese are loyal to their mates. They refuse to leave them, even if their partner is sick or injured. Lately, the geese were everywhere; we talked about how they were so much like us. Mates for life. We'd see them always flying in pairs and it delighted us. Oddly, we even had a pair land right in our yard and walk around on the gravel. I took a photo of two geese marching aimlessly on our driveway. Google Maps error or just spiritual visitors? We commonly saw them doing a flyby, but landing in the yard on our gravel road was just so strange! We couldn't help but think this was another sign.

On a morning walk around Policeman's Creek, we noticed two geese. We watched them and enjoyed their company. It seemed only fitting to spend some of this special time with the geese and enjoy their company. Walking back down the path, we noticed a mature gentleman sitting alone on a bench. At times, he seemed to be talking to himself, which I found odd. He caught my attention with his strange behavior. I said, "Good morning," and without hesitation, he began to make hasty conversation. "I saw two Canada Geese, just over there." Interesting. Now he had our attention. We stopped. I was intrigued by the conversation, and his anxiousness to relay the details.

The grey-haired man in his sixties went on to say how important Canmore was and that it was his first trip back since losing his wife. "We would often sit in this exact spot to watch the geese." Brian and I were both thrown off course with that short conversation. Somehow, it seemed, he was here for *us*. He told us a bit more about how special Canmore was, and then we moved on. As we walked away, we both felt like we should have spent more time with him. We sensed we had just met an angel. This messenger was sent to tell us God was on this journey with us.

Area where we met an angel. Canmore, AB, 2021

SIX: OF GEESE AND ANGELS

Throughout our journey, we encountered several other angels, messengers, or guides. When you're open to receiving them, you have the chance to encounter them. Numerous times at the Cross Cancer Institute, we met or simply crossed paths with angels. I know not everyone will believe this part of our story, and that's okay. The fact that Brian, a no-nonsense kind of guy, believes it and knows that we have experienced the same beautiful energy is all the proof I need.

During a Cross Cancer visit, the course of Brian's treatment plan changed. As we both sat near the pharmacy waiting for Brian's Ozzy pills, we spotted our wonderful pharmacist, Steven. He stopped to chat, asking Brian how he was feeling and proceeding to get an update on the new chemotherapy plan. I was sitting near an elderly gentleman who was wearing an AlPac (Alberta Pacific Forest Industries) jacket. I recognized it because Brian had a similar one about ten years ago. I placed my coffee down on the small side table between us and turned toward Brian and Steven. After about five minutes of conversation, I turned back to grab my coffee. He was gone, but under my coffee sat a beautiful "Coping with Cancer" prayer card. Another moment of wonder. I know the card was not there before I placed my coffee down. The card remains with us today as one of our gifts from our angels.

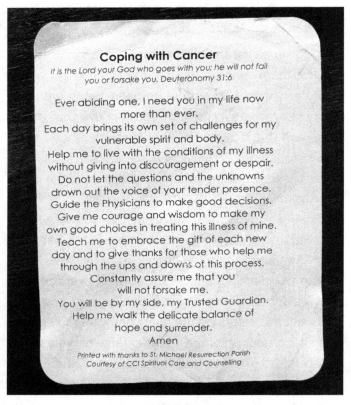

Prayer Card.

Like my mother, I have always felt a deep connection to the spirit world or entities. Maybe that's why God was sending me so many powerful messages. My dreams were also very explicit messages. I had been hearing worship songs all night, almost like the radio was playing music loud and clear. Or sometimes, right in the middle of my sleep, someone's name was shouted in my ear. I've heard that if you wake up hear-

SIX: OF GEESE AND ANGELS

ing music, the angels are singing you to sleep. I began to record the names I heard in the middle of my sleep. After a short while, I opened the notes on my phone and tried to make sense of what it was all about.

Who *were* these people, and why were they so important right now? Were these the names of angels? Claire... Maggie... Glenda... Jerry... Sue... Conal... Lavina... Dylan. After I received the name Conal, it all began to click. These weren't names of angels, but names of their loved ones here on this earth! Their loved ones, who had transcended, were trying to connect with me. I was brought to tears. All these names were somehow given to me by their loved ones who had passed. I wished I could give them more information, but I guess they just wanted me to know that I'd been blessed with the ability to hear their voices. I was in awe. It was a message I heard loud and clear.

Over time, I've shared some of these bizarre experiences with family and close friends. I recall one morning still being asleep in bed when Brian approached me to give me some big news!

"The princess was born."

Before he had a chance to tell me the details, I sleepily responded, "I know, and her name is Charlotte." Puzzled, Brian said, "How did you know that?" I told him, "I had a dream that she was born, and I knew her name."

I can't explain why these things happen to me, but I'm grateful for receiving these gifts.

I know this topic doesn't really relate to anything in our story, but it has helped me to see how closely we are connected to the divine and the spirit world. It also demonstrates that we possess gifts and the ability to connect. I am sure that we've all experienced signs from our loved ones who have passed on. A song, a flickering light, a dragonfly, a rainbow, a feather, or a butterfly.

My mind can clearly recall some of my earliest memories; the sights, smells, or sounds associated with my childhood are very strong. I know I can recall the night my Pepere died, and I would have only been three years old. This was a strong memory, likely attached to the trauma of the situation. He passed at only sixty years old of a sudden heart attack and left his large family in complete devastation. My memory has me standing on the couch as a toddler in our old farmhouse, looking out the window while it rained in the night. Inside, my mother sat on my father's lap, rocking with him as they held each other and cried. She was eight months pregnant and later gave birth to my brother, Aime, named after my deceased grandfather, Aime Michaud. I have shared this memory with my father, but I don't think he wishes to recall that dreadful day.

Years ago, after the passing of my Babka, Brian and I shared a special connection with her. For weeks after her passing, my mom spoke about the light at the bottom of the stairs flickering. While visiting Mom

SIX: OF GEESE AND ANGELS

and Dad, I proceeded to get ready for bed in the basement washroom. I felt a strong tug on the bottom of my nightgown. It was so strong that I literally turned around and looked. It happened one more time, and I giggled. I sensed right away it was Babka, as she loved to tease and had the best laugh. I pictured her laughing as she was playing this joke on me. Later that night, Brian got up to go to the washroom. On his way down the hall, he saw a figure in the bedroom where her items were kept. As he is a no-nonsense kind of guy, he had a hard time believing what he saw but felt, without a doubt, it was her.

I told him nothing of the incident, and he didn't share with me either until our trip to Edmonton the next day. "What are you smiling about?" he asked me. I was actually afraid to tell him because I thought he would think I was strange. He continued to pester me, and finally I gave in and told him about the tug on my nightgown. I will never forget the look on his face. His mouth dropped, and he proceeded to tell me, "I saw her last night when I went to the washroom. I can't explain it, but it was like she was standing in the little room." Without a doubt, she had paid us a visit that night. I prayed for her soul to find peace and rest. I also prayed for her family to mend their differences.

Brian and I continued to receive powerful messages during his cancer battle. On most of our trips to the city, we were gifted with sightings of special birds or animals. Eagles, hawks, owls, moose, fox, and of course, our geese. When you truly put it out into the universe, it will deliver. I ask God for signs that he is close to us, and he responds.

The day Pope Francis visited Edmonton, Brian was home watching TV. He always had the flight app on his phone to track Derek on his numerous journeys. Basically, if you knew the flight number, you could tell the exact departure, location, and destination of the plane. It made for interesting conversation when you saw a plane and could place your bets on its destination. While Brian was watching the CTV Edmonton news at lunch, they mentioned that the Pope was nearby, and then provided his flight number. Brian decided to put it in his flight app—and lo and behold—Pope Francis was flying right above us! Brian was in shock and went out on the deck to listen to the plane above us. He snapped a picture of the flight app details, and it showed the plane right above our home. He shared his exciting news with the family and Father Jhack at the baptism for our great-nephews, Kole and Everett.

Each day, we lit our blessed candle surrounded by the stones of Faith, Hope, Family, Joy, Courage, and Believe. This was one of our rituals, along with our daily prayer and meditation. I always welcomed the angels into our presence and asked them for help. I called the archangels: Raphael, Gabriel, Uriel, and Michael. I know we had so many more angels in our presence, but I called upon these daily and was grateful for their help.

SIX: OF GEESE AND ANGELS

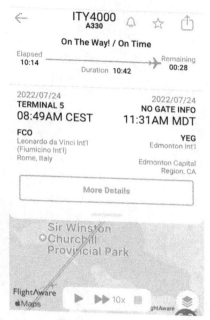

Brian's flight tracker" Lac La Biche, AB, 2022

Our gratitude opens spiritual doors. Maybe this gift will continue to develop through gratitude. As I experience more peace of mind, my ability to express gratitude grows. Learning to give it to God has brought me an indescribable peace.

Do not be anxious about anything, but in every situation, by prayer and petition, with thanksgiving, present your requests to God. And the peace of God, which transcends all understanding, will guard your hearts and your minds in Christ Jesus. (Philippians 4:6-7, NIV)

Seven
Find Hope, Keep Hope, Build Hope

SHORTLY AFTER BRIAN'S diagnosis and during the pandemic, our local school division introduced a campaign of "Hope." Well, wasn't that perfect timing! Signs of hope sprung up all over our community. We couldn't have asked for a better theme to surround ourselves with. They say we each have a purpose, and I began to see that my purpose was exactly this: to find hope, keep hope, and build hope wherever possible. I decided to add one more title to my resume: Hope Mentor.

We adopted this as our personal motto and inspiration. I was planting hope everywhere I could. This message was about to go out everywhere. Hope would be heard loud and clear. Regardless of each and every battle we faced with this disease, we would remain hopeful and believe in "Every Perfect Possibility."

I paste hoped cards in our house; students and coworkers sent messages of hope; family and friends showered us with hope. We were engulfed in a hope-filled spirit, and I planned to maintain this. We made a meditation/prayer room which we called our Hope Room. We adorned it with messages and items of hope: the Archangel Raphael, birds, a cross, dream catchers, rock art, wedding memorabilia, and a sign that read "Expect Miracles." I wondered, was it that easy to just "expect" a miracle?

JAWS/Interact students planting hope

Where Do You Find Hope?
It's not like we can just go into the store and buy hope, so it is very important to know where to find it. I find hope in nature, touching the dirt, hearing the birds, seeing the sunrise, smelling the fresh air after a rain.

SEVEN: FIND HOPE, KEEP HOPE, BUILD HOPE

Life is truly a gift. When you learn to appreciate each day and its blessings, you will find hope everywhere. As a career counsellor, I have read many articles about the importance of hope in determining students' success. A person without hope is like a sinking ship without a life raft. Hope is our buoyancy; it keeps us afloat regardless of high waters, tides, and storms. Without hope we are most certain to sink. This doesn't mean that we die, but we will never truly live with joy believing in all life's possibilities. Having hope builds resilience. It's like carrying a superpower around. No matter what comes your way, you have the tools to handle the situation.

I find hope in children and animals. Fortunately for us, our family was full of little humans. These precious, gentle, innocent souls were such incredible gifts. More than ever, we realized we needed these little people in our lives. They lifted our spirits and shared so much love and light. Similar to those little blessings, we were also blessed with a special friend— Hercules, our dog. From the time of Brian's diagnosis, Hercules not only shared his love but became a wonderful distraction. His love and energy were a true blessing. We are forever grateful for his affection as it not only made us accountable to his needs but receptive to all the joy he brought.

Doodling with Aubrey. St. Lina Camp, AB, 2023

"Little Miracles"
Great-nephews Kole and Everett, 2022

SEVEN: FIND HOPE, KEEP HOPE, BUILD HOPE

Another way to find hope is through community. The first Terry Fox Run during Covid was virtual, so we registered Team Breathe Hope. Brian and I were able to do six kilometres and take this photo. We raised nine hundred dollars for the foundation. I prayed that this drop in the bucket would bring us that one piece of missing information to solve cancer for everyone inflicted with this disease.

Team Breathe Hope Begins" Lisa and Brian, 2021

I never considered losing my walking partner. Oh, the miles we had travelled and places we had discovered. After his brain tumour diagnosis and radiation, Brian lost much of the mobility and strength in his right leg, making distance walking a challenging task. This was probably the most difficult adjustment for both of us. The inability to walk together brought much sadness.

"Team Breathe Hope crew"
Terry Fox Run, Lac La Biche, AB, 2022

"Team Breathe Hope"
Lisa, Brian, Max, and children, 2023

SEVEN: FIND HOPE, KEEP HOPE, BUILD HOPE

We will not give up on believing that, one day, Brian's ability to walk will be restored.

We also found hope in God and through prayer. Although we did not attend church, our days began and ended in prayer. I took to reading Scripture and listening to spiritual podcasts. It brought us comfort to feel connected to God. It centred us and brought us a profound peace.

How Do You Keep Hope?

Keeping hope is about remaining positive even when life presents challenges. At times, it feels like it's challenge upon challenge. Hope is closely connected to our faith. I believe if we do not have faith, we cannot have hope. The two just belong together: hope plus faith. It's a peas and carrots kind of relationship. Remaining positive is absolutely necessary, although it's not easy. Several times in the battle, I found my mind wandering into those deep, dark, scary places. I reminded myself to breathe and take it one day at a time. Looking too far ahead with any disease does you no good. It takes personal strength but also prayer and community to help get you through those turbulent times.

We were so fortunate to have the love and support of family, friends, and our community. When we would lose hope, we'd borrow it from some of those amazing people and their prayers and messages. I firmly believe that community is a huge factor in healing. Community is that group of people who lift you up and have you, no matter what! We were extremely grateful for our community. To this day, I consider them our extended family.

My sister Marcy and niece Danika raised funds for us through an online auction called "Brian's Battle." The support of this event was incredible and heartwarming. They put a tremendous amount of work into receiving and processing donations for the event. It was emotionally overwhelming for us to even watch the event progress. The money it raised has helped so much with appointment costs, travel expenses, and some of the consultation and biopsy costs at the Dana Farber Hospital. We were so grateful to our loving family and friends for their support, as well as the community who opened their arms to receive us and create such a successful event. Your love and generosity will never be forgotten.

Later in the journey, our beautiful friend Max took to the road and embarked on a long, treacherous run for Brian. It didn't surprise me one bit to see her step up and bring her strength, faith, and determination into our circle of support. Max began training early and also recruited support for us. She had a logo made for Brian's Battle, and we saw the shirts all over the region, from Bonnyville to Lac La Biche and beyond. It was another powerful example of community at work. We asked Max to share the proceeds from her run with two local cancer charities, Haying in the 30s and Road to Hope. She surpassed her goal and raised over ten thousand dollars for us and these local charities. Serving others

SEVEN: FIND HOPE, KEEP HOPE, BUILD HOPE

this way was an important part of our healing plan. Thankfully, Max did all the running! What an incredible friend.

I recalled many times throughout our marriage when we would hear of individuals needing help. Brian would say, "Just give it to them." Even if we needed the money, it was important that the people who needed it more were looked after. To this day, whenever we hear of a need or know we can be of service, we feel a deep desire to make a difference. The more light you share, the brighter the world will be.

How Do You Build Hope?
If you can find hope and keep hope, you can build hope! I see hope-building as the everyday things we can do to elevate our circumstances. Early on in our journey, after reading several articles and books, we implemented things that would maintain our *hope practice.*

1. *Prayer*: God First plan. Begin each day in prayer and with gratitude. End each day with prayer and a thankful heart. Some people may choose meditation time, but for us it was prayer that meant so much and provided peace and calm.
2. *Mindfulness*: Remove the fluffy stuff. Focus on gratitude and live in the moment. Take things moment by moment, day by day. Be present. Hold yourself to the present, not to past regrets or worry about the future.

3. *Goals*: Set short- and long-term goals. Write down and share your dreams for the future. Call it a bucket list, and make sure it means something to you. It truly isn't about the material possessions, but the experience and meaning and memories behind the adventure.
4. *Connection*: Develop relationships with God, your family, and your support community. Allow the community to support you when you need it. Within connection is service; it is our responsibility as beings on this earth to help others.
5. *Trust*: Release control of the situation, and *give it to God.* Trust that God wants you well and that *no miracle* is too big for him!
6. *Vision*: Create a vision board to reflect your goals and aspirations. Believe in every perfect possibility. Post items that reflect the hope all around you. Don't forget to include your bucket list.

Our Vision Board" 2021

SEVEN: FIND HOPE, KEEP HOPE, BUILD HOPE

7. *Intentions:* Set your healing intentions. Believe that you have the power within you to heal. God has given you this gift. Jesus died to give us the gift of eternal life, forgiveness, and healing.
8. *Quiet*: Learn to appreciate and embrace the quiet. Even if you have to get up early! I have found so much peace in the morning, reflecting on God's Word while watching the sky awake and the birds gather. In the words of Chief Dan George, "The greatest wisdom is found in silence, for it allows us to truly listen."[3]
9. *Positivity*: Remain positive and know that miracles happen. The more positive energy you put out, the more positive you receive.
10. *Gratitude*: Begin each day with a grateful heart. Wake up and open your heart. Share your gratitude and love with others so they can feel your incredible energy.
11. *Forgiveness*: Ask, accept, give, and receive forgiveness. Negative emotions all originate from fear. Letting go of guilt, anger, pain, shame, sadness, resentment, remorse, and grief are critical to healing the mind and body.

May the God of hope fill you with all joy and peace as you trust in him, so that you may overflow with hope by the power of the Holy Spirit. (Romans 15:13, NIV)

Eight
Scans, Scans, and More Tumours!!

AFTER SIX MONTHS stable, Brian's scans show increased tumour activity in the brain. Our oncologist was hopeful that Brian could be a candidate for Gamma Knife radiation, which can target up to eight single tumours with precise execution. Things were on the move quickly, and within a week, we were referred to the Gamma Knife team at the University of Alberta hospital and had a date for scan and treatment. As with a heart attack, time was a huge factor, so we were pleased that things got underway so quickly. Once again, Brian's unshakeable spirit and determination to be well was put to the test. We prayed that God would lead our healing journey and direct the actions of our doctors.

The night before the Gamma Knife appointment, we checked into a hotel near the hospital. At the front desk, a young man pulled up our reservation. As Brian checked us in, I noticed the spelling of his name on the reservation card: *Brain*. Hmm... interesting, right? I prayed this was a good sign. The night was cold, windy, and extremely long. We did our best to rest and be ready for a long and difficult day.

In the morning, the hospital settled us in a quiet glass room, in and among other Gamma Knife patients. Some looked well, but we couldn't help noticing others with very sad and frail appearances. One slight man in his forties sat across from us; he appeared so weak. I sensed such deep despair and hopelessness that my heart ached for him. I was thankful we were feeling strong and that Brian had such an incredible warrior spirit. God's Got Ya!

Brian was taken in for an MRI to help them assess and plan his Gamma Knife treatment. He was brought back quickly. I had spent that time in prayer. For a long while, we waited as others around us seemed to be moving ahead. I started to panic and my mind was troubled. I couldn't pray anymore. I felt sick. I know I've written about not falling victim to fear, but there were times like this when I felt so helpless and afraid. I could feel it in my heart that something was not right.

Two doctors, a female and a male, approached our room and began to share more bad news. They apologized and said that, unfortunately, Brian was not a candidate for the Gamma Knife treatment. He had too many small tumours scattered throughout his brain. How could this be? Just eight weeks ago there was only one, yet now they described the tumours

EIGHT: SCANS, SCANS, AND MORE TUMOURS!

as "peppered" throughout his brain. Seriously? "Brian, you will need whole brain radiation. You are not a candidate for Gamma." She continued to explain that, sometimes, you needed to clean it up. The plan had changed again. We would return to the radiation department for ten sessions of whole brain radiation. It was the most harsh and intrusive way to do a clean sweep of the brain and those nasty tumours. *Was it like wiping a computer clean?* I wondered. *Wiping out every memory and part of him and our beautiful life?* We were left with so many questions and concerns.

Once again, we felt overwhelmed and defeated. My stomach was upset and nauseous. How would this change Brian? And had we truly reached the end of this battle? I admit this was one of our weakest and most desperate times. How could this be God's plan? Why couldn't things just work out in our favor? Right then, our hope was depleted, and so too was our faith. This would be a very difficult treatment, and again we'd have to explain this bad news to all our loved ones who were waiting and praying for positive results from the Gamma Knife appointment. *God, you could have made this so much easier for us. Why are you still testing us? What more do you want us to do or learn? Are we not worthy of your healing?*

Treatment for whole brain radiation was set for March 2022. Our plans to attend Derek's dentistry convocation in Ireland were now out the window. There were so many unknowns about how Brian would come through this treatment. How would it affect his personality, memory, vision, hearing, or mobility? Prayers went up, for strength and for our hope and faith to be restored. It felt like we'd reached our lowest low. I wasn't sure we'd recover from this blow.

Derek's Dentistry Grad
University of Cork, Ireland, 2022

Nine
Passing Time

SOMETIMES, I JUST cannot comprehend where the time has gone. With everything that's taken place over the last few years—and adding in the COVID factor—it seems like a big, muddled mess. It's difficult to keep different points of time straight, and all the events that have taken place sometimes fall out of order. While writing this book I've asked Brian questions like, When did the brain radiation take place? When was it that we went to the mountains? When did you get the last CT scan? Thankfully, Brian is phenomenal with details and has it recorded in the notes in his phone. One quick check and he helps to set me on course.

How can you be "retired" but busy all the time? Our retirement plan is a little different than we ever pictured. First, it came about ten years before it was supposed to! Calling it retirement at least makes us feel like we've reached this milestone together in our lives. I know Brian would have been a difficult guy to convince it was time to retire. Not only did he love his job and the people he worked with, but he had also found his purpose. As a planner, his skills shone. He'd found what he believed was his calling: organizing, assessing, managing, and distributing the workload to staff and contractors to keep his area of the mill running in tip-top shape. Even having to leave his job, it was difficult for him not to think about his work. To this day, his home office remains intact, and I am sure he's just waiting for the time to "fire up" again!

Once we'd settled into our new routine, it was easy for the days to quickly pass. I soon realized that we needed to be focused and accountable for how we spent our time; otherwise, the hours would slip away into days and weeks. Thank goodness the New York Times only releases one Wordle a day! Our first priority was always prayer and God, but often the week would be organized around appointment schedules. Keeping a list of what needed to happen that week and where we were going. Brian was great at handling all the details and even kept me posted on my appointments! Some weeks were very busy with tests, doctors, and appointments, but other times we were free! I tried to find little projects around the house that Brian could help with, things to give us a sense of accomplishment. Over time, this slipped and I had to refocus. No, guys, this was not a Honey Do List—just my attempt to keep us engaged and feeling productive.

NINE: PASSING TIME

I had taken up rock art. I don't even know how it happened, but it definitely helped to fill the void. Our office became my rock room, and I actually organized my rocks to make creating projects a little easier for me. I made gifts for my family and friends, and even commissioned a few pieces. It was a nice creative getaway from all the cancer stuff.

Looking back now, I feel it's very important to have a hobby like this in retirement or during cancer treatment. A creative outlet provides a healthy venue that's free from worry or judgment. I felt close to the rocks. They each meant something to me, and as I built these projects, it was easy to lose my sense of time. A big part of making these projects was being able to give something of myself to others, those that I loved and cared about. The first Christmas I began my rock art, I was pumping them out like Santa's workshop! They maybe weren't the best of my work, but they were from the heart, and all of the projects came about easily, as if the rocks were waiting for me to just pick them and put them together. Lately, my rocks have been sitting without any attention. It's not that I won't go back to them, but I've switched gears and have begun writing our story. This takes up my creative time and energy.

Brian and I were fortunate enough to work on a creative project together in the summer of 2023. We home took the old farm sign and replenished it for Mom and Dad. This was truly a labour of love. It was extra special because it was also something Brian had a hand in creating with me. I am proud of our work, and it was even more amazing to watch *him* work. Although this was out of his element, Brian applied the same focus and effort he did to all his tasks. He was far better at the fine detail painting than I was!

"Michaud Sign Project" 2023

Brian and I have been blessed with the time to pursue adventure. Our bucket list includes many more places we wish to travel and see, but it has become a challenge given treatment, health, and mobility issues. We certainly tried our best, and following whole brain radiation, Brian and I planned a short getaway to Victoria. Although this trip did present some issues with how Brian was feeling, we made the best of it, and I would love to travel back to this spot under different circumstances to fully embrace the experience. I'm convinced the next trip to Victoria is going to be in June or July so we can avoid that cold, chilled-to-the-bone seaside factor.

"The ocean, his happy place"
Brentwood Bay, B.C., 2022

Having this time together was truly a blessing. Whether we were just hanging out at home or travelling to new or old places, God had given us this incredible gift. Short excursions within Alberta, British Columbia, and Saskatchewan have helped us re-energize and provided strength for the next leg of the journey. I'm so grateful we travelled when it was possible, and I'm even more grateful for the memories we made on our journey. It may seem different right now, but I am hopeful that we'll be able to enjoy many new travel experiences again.

Brian at Athabasca Falls, Jasper, AB, 2023

NINE: PASSING TIME

In September 2023, we jumped in our vehicle and drove to Highway 11, the David Thompson Highway, which separates Banff and Jasper. It has the most amazing views. This short trip was a redo from a previous excursion in 2006. Most of the way, I handled the drive, although Brian took over for some of the white-knuckle points. Crazy to think I let him take the wheel even with a bad leg!

Ten

God Can Do the Impossible

FROM THE BEGINNING of our journey, we surrounded ourselves with messages of miracles and hope. Our family and friends reminded us that miracles were possible. I was browsing through a local hardware store when a sign "Expect Miracles" appeared before me. I picked it up. What if we just expected a miracle? Was it that easy? Could we expect a miracle and then God would deliver it? On the spot, I put an order in for that supersized miracle, delivery required!

One of the first stories I read after diagnosis was about George. George was terminally ill and had six months to live. Those were just statistics, though. What of the man, and what of miracles and God's work? His family asked the doctor, "Should we tell him the facts so he can deal with the reality of his situation?" The doctor pondered and reflected, "But what truly is his reality? For each ten, one survives; for each thousand, one hundred will live!" Although George knew his diagnosis, he was never given the bleak prognosis. He was a man who defied the odds. Unknowingly, he went on to live many more years in remission after his treatments.

So what would have happened if George had been told he had six months to live? Would he have lived more than six months? I believe that if he'd been given this news, George would have likely died. Call it the placebo effect, but I do believe that healing the body is possible, and there have been many cases of radical remission. Brian always says, "My body made it, my body can heal it!" If we look again at *The Biology of Belief*, Dr. Lipton describes the wonderment of the placebo effect, serving as evidence of just how powerful our minds are. They have the capacity to truly heal our bodies. Early on in diagnosis, we watched the documentary *Healed* with our friends Bill and Brenda. It showed case after case of what the medical community would call "healing miracles." People healed themselves of their critical and deadly illnesses.

There is no such thing as false hope. Hope is hope, but where does it come from? We have already discussed the topic of hope, but what if you truly feel that God's got you? Throughout this journey, I can honestly say that God has told me not to worry and that he has got us. There has always been this quiet confidence that we're going to be okay. How can I even begin to believe that, against all odds, Brian will beat this? I

TEN: GOD CAN DO THE IMPOSSIBLE

can. I know this man. Despite every difficult part of this journey, I will continue to believe that there exists a power to change our circumstances. A power that can bring a healing miracle. I hold onto this hope.

For Christmas 2022, Brian bought me a "Believe Bird," a small chickadee ornament with the word *Believe* written under it. As winter in Alberta finally faded away, we got the pleasure of enjoying so many birds at the feeder, one our favourites being the special chickadees. Early one morning, Brian was sitting at the couch and a poor little chickadee hit our large window and dropped. He stepped outside to examine it and, although the bird still seemed to be alive, it did not look promising. When I woke up, Brian told me that he'd picked it up and placed it by a tree in the yard. We gave it some time. Brian warned me that he didn't think it would survive. I was deeply upset by this. Some people might think I'm irrational, but that morning it was devastating news.

We gave our special believe bird time to recover and then walked out to the tree together. He was still and unmoving. His precious little eyes were open, and he looked so afraid, stunned, and lost. My heart ached as Brian contemplated putting it out of its misery. We saw him move his wings, and I closed my eyes in prayer. Somehow, I felt that if this bird died, so would my strength, my power to believe. I actually cried for this little bird, and Brian said, "Okay, we'll give it a bit more time and check later this afternoon."

The afternoon came, and from our deck, we could still see him sitting in the same spot. Dead or alive, he hadn't moved. Our youngest son, Travis, went to check and told us his eyes were open but thought maybe he was brain dead. Brian went down to reassess. I knew Travis was upset by the bird situation too. He was so passionate about animals and always has been. At one point, as a child, he didn't want to eat meat. Chicken really upset him. When you roast a whole chicken, you definitely know what you're eating! When he was about eight years old, he asked what we were having for supper? I told him it was chicken, and then he responded, "Is it an old chicken or a young chicken?" An old one. Okay, he agreed to eat it! I guess Travis felt it was acceptable to eat an old chicken. What a kid, he truly fills our hearts, and although so much younger than his brothers, he came into our life at just the perfect time!

This journey has brought us all closer together. I am especially proud of the time and attention our boys give to their dad. Scott's daily calls and conversations are about vehicles, politics, recipes, renovations, and work. They really enjoy each other's company, and they are so much alike. Derek enjoys cooking and baking for his dad, especially all his favourites like eggs Benny and crème brûlée. Now that he's home, Derek can have Brian's advice. They have discussions about politics, finances, history, vehicles, hockey, and cur-

TEN: GOD CAN DO THE IMPOSSIBLE

rent events. There isn't a topic you can pull out of a hat that Brian hasn't read about.

Travis, our youngest, graduated high school and was ready to begin Police Studies at MacEwan University in the fall. As much as I would have chosen a different path for Travis; Brian was adamant that it was his decision, and we would support him as we did his brothers with their career plans. He loves spending time with Travis, watching YouTubers, Marvel movies, and the Mandalorian series. They spend quality time discussing the process and the storyline. Both are serious Star Wars fans and share many similar movie interests.

I watched from a distance as Brian and Travis inspected our believe bird. I began to pray and asked God to heal our little bird. I had my eyes closed in prayer when Brian yelled, "There he goes. He just flew to the tree!" Brian had picked up a stick and used it to gently coax him to move. Suddenly, he was up, up, and away! *Thank you, Lord, for healing our little bird.*

Several times after that, I would see a chickadee land at our feeder and think, *Is it our little bird?* One day a few months later in Bonnyville, while Brian was being assessed for treatment, a chickadee actually flew and landed right on our windowpane. Brian caught my attention and pointed; the little one just sat and looked at us as we returned the same level of admiration. I would keep on believing that God could do this, that God's got us. I would remain patient.

Believe Bird, Gift from Brian, Christmas 2022

Eleven
Chemo Has Come

AFTER A LONG and difficult winter, our friends and neighbours, Bill and Brenda, had planned a month in Loreto, Mexico. We discussed plans to join them, and I was hopeful we could spend this time together making memories in a much warmer climate. We were so grateful to all the people who had literally lifted us up: family, friends, medical staff, colleagues, and community members. We received so much support from them and our family during these ups and downs; I don't know how we could have survived this roller coaster ride without all our care bears.

Brian received news about his scans before Christmas 2022 and said, "I'm taking you to Mexico!" A thrilling statement. We come home to tell Bill and Brenda we were going to join them for a week in Loreto. Brenda and I shared a big hug and some tears. We were going to Mexico, and it was going to be amazing!

The scan results were wishy-washy; everything appeared somewhat stable, but there always seemed to be hot spots. More uptake in T11 and the left iliac crest, but nothing major. I guess our definition of major had changed over the past twenty-two months.

A Cold One, Loreto Bay, MX, 2023

Loreto was a great experience for us but also a challenging time. I remembered the days when a vacation meant hours of sitting in the sunshine, sipping margaritas, partying in nightclubs, and covering miles of beach as we walked along the ocean. This time we rented a

ELEVEN: CHEMO HAS COME

golf cart to help Brian get along on the longer walks. He managed a couple good days and about nine thousand steps, which was pretty awesome. At this time, his leg was weak but still useful. We both struggled with our energy levels. I think when you're always on high alert and in fight mode, it's hard to transition your body into relaxation. It literally shuts off. As always, Bill and Brenda were great hosts and made adjustments to their schedule to make it nice and easy for us.

A Special Friendship -
Brenda, Bill, Lisa, and Brian, 2023

One of the great memories we shared with them was a phone call from Derek. We FaceTimed with him regularly to see how things were going. Derek had been waiting for nine weeks to hear about his dental exam results—his board exam. It had been a stressful time for him as he needed this last piece in place to begin practicing as a dentist. After some small talk about hockey, politics, and the vacation, Derek said, "Oh, by the way, I passed the boards!" I began crying, a happy release that he had met all the requirements for practicing as a Canadian dentist. It had been a long, stressful, and emotional roller coaster. He had persevered. I knew that, as much as he'd wanted this for himself, he'd wanted it for his dad too!

After a relaxing vacation in Mexico, we returned home to more winter weather and prepared for the next set of scans. Following scans, there was always a waiting period to meet with the oncologist. Often Brian's results were posted on his health portal prior to seeing the doctor. There were times we read them and other times we avoided it. Errors in understanding, or misunderstandings, have occurred and cost us precious amounts of rest.

Brian's appointment arrived. Our doctor came into the room and said, "Have you read your scans?" He is just like that, forthright and frank. We needed him to be a part of our team, and we needed to trust him. There were times we thought we would try to switch doctors, but we were always hesitant. You don't want to burn any bridges when you're a patient in a healthcare crisis, post-Covid. He seemed very competent, but we could not let his nature dampen our spirits. This time we said, no, we hadn't read the scans, and

ELEVEN: CHEMO HAS COME

he proceeded to say there were a number of spots popping up. Brian's lymph nodes were also "juicy," meaning they were plump. There were also concerns about the brain, the bones (specifically T11), and one possible new site in the lungs. The doctor said, "I think it's time for chemotherapy. Some doctors may have argued that I've waited too long".

With a marker, he wrote down the different types of chemo on a whiteboard. He presented two options: either Cisplatin plus Pemetrexed or Carboplatin plus Pemetrexed. We felt he was asking us to choose. But how were we supposed to know what was best for Brian? The doctor didn't really offer an opinion; it was bizarre to think that he wouldn't provide a recommendation. We needed some assurance of the best way to proceed. The first thing we'd do at home was contact our doctor at the Dana Farber Hospital to get his opinion.

Chemotherapy gets a bad rap. We've all heard the horror stories about it. Killing your good cells to eliminate cancer. Is there no other way to handle this disease? Many argue that there are better ways to beat it. Some find success in natural treatments and holistic methods. Some travel to Mexico for treatment. Brian was well-read, but he still chose to place his chips on science and research. While we did this, we prayed each day for God to direct us down the right healing path. We also prayed it was his will for Brian to be healed of this terrible disease.

One morning, while checking the Facebook sites we monitored for patient information, I read that two of the cancer warriors we followed had lost their battles. Sadly, one was Matt, a young man from Calgary, Alberta. Matt had chosen a more natural protocol. His journey began with a large brain tumour and surgery. Later, it was discovered that he also had non-small cell lung cancer with the EGFR mutation. Somehow, like Brian, they were able to determine that the primary tumour was in his lungs. Matt left behind two young children and a legacy to fight this terrible disease.

Early in our cancer journey, I spent so much time thinking about what to do and where to turn for treatment. Everyone offered great advice and I never took this for granted. In my mind I thought, *What about prayer and believing and trusting in God's healing? I feel God directing us to the right treatment, at the right time, for the right reason. Brian is healing; be patient, Lisa. God is listening, and it will come.*

Back home, a quick email to Boston was followed by a return phone call. A nurse practitioner from our doctor's office at Dana Farber called to inform us that the best practice and standard of care at their hospital is Carbo plus Pemetrexed. She assured us that, of the thirteen doctors working in this specialized unit, all of them preferred this chemo plan because the other had harsher side effects. It wasn't easy to make this choice, but having their expertise certainly made us feel more confident about the next steps.

ELEVEN: CHEMO HAS COME

We told our family and friends about the chemo. It was a scary time. Anytime you have to access another treatment, you feel like your options are running out. We hoped and prayed for more treatments to be available in the future as research improved, and doctors gained a better understanding of this type of cancer. For now, we left the rest in God's hands.

In February 2023, Brian and I travelled to Bonnyville, one of the local cancer care centres, for his first of four treatments. This would be followed by a maintenance treatment of pemetrexed. If everything went as planned, Brian would have his regular treatments completed before Travis graduated high school at the end of June. The doctors and nurses were amazing, and we felt at ease and comfortable in our new surroundings. Volunteers brought warm handmade quilts, lunch, and tea. You can not beat that small town hospitality!

On our first day, we met a lovely local doctor. She was very knowledgeable and so positive. This was a comforting change from the time-pressed doctor at the CCI. In Bonnyville, the doctors are trained in cancer care, but they are not oncologists. It felt good to be in a facility that was less busy and more patient centred. After examining Brian and reviewing his case, she gave the green light for treatment in a couple of days. Before we left her office, she said something that has stuck with me. "Cancer is changing. There are a lot of people who will die *with* cancer but not *from* cancer."

She informed Brian that he had a lot of life to live. God bless her. I needed to hear that.

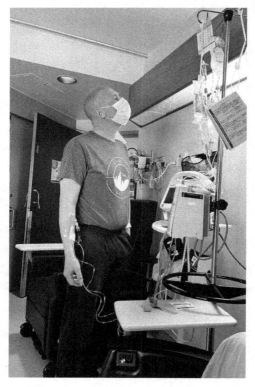

Brian inspects his chemo meds,
Bonnyville Cancer Centre, 2023

The Bonnyville Cancer Centre became a place of hope and healing. All the nursing staff and volunteers, as well as our doctors, were a vital part of Brian's healing team. We were so incredibly thankful that they were part of our journey.

ELEVEN: CHEMO HAS COME

Snowy Owl quilt by Isabelle, Brian and Isabelle, 2023

I sought the Lord, and he heard me, and delivered me from all my fears. (Psalm 34:4, NKJV)

Twelve
A Complicated Mess

SOMETIMES THINGS ARE just complicated. There's no other way to describe this next set of circumstances. Treatments, side effects, treatments, hospitals, treatments, worry, hospitals, tests. I have always said that my life has been a complicated mess. If you wanted to go on a great ride, jump on my adversity roller coaster! My family has certainly seen our share of crisis and trauma. We sometimes go about life thinking that we are the only ones experiencing all this sadness and misfortune; we have blinders on. The truth is, each of us, at one point or another, will take a ride on the adversity roller coaster. That is precisely why it's so important to have a solid tool kit to deal with the stuff life might throw at you. This experience was truly an opportunity for us to process some of the pain from the past and grow stronger in our faith today.

Life may feel the same for you, as you run around and manage the day-to day-stuff while having one setback after another. That's exactly how I felt this next part of the journey was going for us. We were busy getting through one little hiccup after another. It was literally one hiccup after another! Did you know when the body is dehydrated, or the brain is irritated, you will have a lot of hiccups? Anytime Brian was on his steroids for treatment, he had an incredible case of the hiccups. Maybe it was just the challenges of chemotherapy and all the new medications, but we were experiencing far too many hiccups!

Chemotherapy has been used to treat cancer since the 1950s, and they seem to have figured out a way to minimize its side effects. Prior to chemo, Brian was on a regiment of meds to hopefully mitigate these problems. He began medications to deal with the nasty side effects associated with it: nausea, vomiting, rash, diarrhea, fatigue. One of the meds he was on again was a steroid. While undergoing brain radiation, Brian had been on a very heavy dose of dexamethasone. Despite its advantage to reduce swelling in the brain, it was a difficult drug to manage. This time the dex would be used to help with rash, nausea, and inflammation. The side effects were many, and strange things began to pop up. We were left chasing our tails, trying to figure out what was causing the issues. Was it the chemotherapy, the targeted therapy pill (Ozzy), or the dex? For someone who rarely took medication, his body was overloaded with toxic junk.

TWELVE: A COMPLICATED MESS

Brian seemed to be managing the chemo well. He started to put on weight and looked stronger. Randomly, he developed a dark mark on his foot, with tenderness, redness, and swelling. We ended up in the emergency unit. This was one of many times we had to see the doctor during his course of chemotherapy. It was always difficult to explain everything going on, and it was hard to know where to begin with a new doctor. Luckily, it was our doctor on call. We felt very fortunate to have her expertise and knowledge to help sort through this cancer conundrum. Tests were ordered to rule out DVT (blood clot) as well as to check bloodwork. By the time they determine that everything was fine, the mark and pain had disappeared.

Several similar incidents happened throughout the period of a few months of treatment. It was challenging and draining on us. It was especially hard on Brian, who was trying so hard to stay positive and strong. We were both thankful to have reached the point in time we could watch Travis graduate from high school. As I look back to the day of diagnosis, I realize there were many times on the adversity roller coaster when I was afraid Brian would not be there with us. Travis graduated from high school, and we are able to celebrate the day with our family. But by the end of the evening, Brian's feet were so huge that his dress shoes no longer fit.

The following day he was back in the emergency room. They prescribed a water pill, and ordered tests on his heart, lungs, and kidneys. Thankfully, he passed them all with flying colours. It was a great feeling, but it was frustrating to not have any solid answers. The local cancer doctors consulted with our oncologist, and everyone was stumped—unable to explain or provide a reason for such terrible swelling. The process of elimination began. Was it the chemotherapy, Ozzy, or dex? While all this was going on, we were still trying to sort out why Brian had lost so much mobility in his right leg. Day after day, it seemed to be weakening. I just wished God would give us a break and cut us some slack.

Lord, help us to sort out this mess. Help guide us and the doctors to the answers and treatments Brian needs. Cancer is difficult enough without all the other crazy symptoms going on!

Our Daily Cancer Prayer
Cancer, you are dead.
I command you out of my body in Jesus' name.
Cancer, you are leaving my body now.
I graciously release you.
Thank you for the gifts you have given us.
It is time for you to leave.

TWELVE: A COMPLICATED MESS

"Grad 2023" Scott, Brianna, Mischa, Travis, Lisa, Brian, and Derek. In front of Julie's 1932 Ford Coupe

"Proud Parents" Travis's Grad, 2023

Daily Healing Affirmations:

I am Strong
I am Healthy
I am Healed
I am Safe
Healthy lungs, cancer-free lungs
Healthy brain, cancer-free brain
Healthy bones, cancer-free bones.
Later, we would add:
Healthy leg, strong leg,
strong muscles and nerves.

Thirteen
North to Alaska

IN APRIL 2023, we decided to book a cruise to Alaska. This year was our thirtieth wedding anniversary, and although we celebrated our twenty-ninth at a campout with family and friends, we wanted to do something special this time, for us. I recruited the company of my brother Herve and his special friend, Julie, to travel with us. I felt so much better having them along, in case the waters got rough, and I had to manage health issues with Brian. They gave us a sense of security and support.

Brian was scheduled for scans right before we left at the end of July. He was also scheduled for treatment at that time. We had always wanted to take a cruise, and going to Alaska through the inside passage was going to be amazing! Given his health conditions, we took all the insurance possible, which added a hefty price to the trip. But it would all be worth it. We were really excited about this adventure and the opportunity to add a new destination to our travel map.

Brian delayed chemotherapy treatment by two weeks but proceeded with his scans a few days prior to our departure. We decided not to look at any of the results while vacationing in Alaska. Again, his leg was clumsy and weak. There had been little improvement with this, and we could both see it was getting worse. As we were boarding the ship, we both felt nervous about the size of the vessel. Brian had been struggling to get around on solid ground; is this cruise going to be too much for him to handle? So far, he was managing without a cane or walker.

The excitement built when we saw the ship—it was so awesome! A grand experience and such a thrill. Brian always watched these shows on TV about amazing engineering and structures; this was definitely one to marvel at! Cancer had manifested such a different mental and emotional level of gratitude for us. Eyes were wide open, and we were mindful with appreciation for each and every moment and experience. Despite our challenges, there were still days where God's grace filled us with a peace beyond understanding. He lived within us, and we were within him. Realizing this brought us deep joy and fulfillment.

Our trip was amazing—what an absolutely perfect time of wonder and blessing. We were told that mild weather was quite unusual for a cruise to Alaska, but we were so fortunate to experience all this beauty at

THIRTEEN: NORTH TO ALASKA

sea with the most amazing weather. Still, I found myself looking around the room and wondering if there was anyone else here who fighting the same battle we were. You always feel alone when you have cancer, yet we knew, based on statistics, that there were many people in the room that had it then or had experienced it in the past. Some were obvious, like the lady with her head cover and painted eyebrows. But there were likely many others who were trying to live life to its fullest and were in the same cancer battle.

On day four of our trip, Brian's feet began to swell again. Tempted to cancel our day excursion in Skagway, we assessed the risks. This was the one trip Brian was really wanting to go on. We could not miss it— we wouldn't! The adventure of the Klondike train up the White Pass Summit was something he had been looking forward to. Deciding to go for it, we managed to get there; we randomly sat on the left side of the train car. I could tell Brian was thrilled to be on the old train and get a window seat, which was fine with me. I had never been a fan of heights. Being that we were planning to tackle the White Pass Summit, I could only imagine this might mean I'd be white knuckled! No matter the trauma, I would do it because, if anyone deserved this experience, it was him.

A narrow old train car crept up the summit, moving us from Alaska back over the Canadian border. Along the way, we were blessed with beautiful, yet frightening, sites. Several times during the trip, Brian asked me to look out the window. It felt like we were hanging off the edge of the mountain. I'd take a quick glimpse and then retreat to my aisle space. My safe zone. I even felt my body trying to shift the whole train to the right on the inside of the mountain passage. Later, I realized I wasn't the only one who was uncomfortable with the train and the heights we are travelling at. Behind us was a couple from B.C., and she was at the window. Like me, a big burly man beside her leaned his body to the right, hoping the two of us could keep this train car on an even keel! It was comical, both of our spouses begging us to look out the window, while without hesitation, we passed and took deep breaths. I was glad it was a foggy day. I couldn't really see what lay below us!

That night we returned to the ship, and Brian was resting in the room, his feet swollen again. After he fell asleep, I was restless and feeling overwhelmed. I decided to walk down to the main cafeteria and get some tea. In my favourite, comfy pjs, I met Don, who was also looking for a warm drink late in the evening. We got into a conversation about the trip, and I discovered that he was a retired RCMP officer and CSIS agent. How awesome! What a fascinating career he'd had. Not wanting to miss an opportunity, I discussed the future career of our youngest son, Travis, who planned to be a police officer. Immediately, we formed a bond. At one point in the conversation, I told Don about Brian, and I guess my emotions took over. The

THIRTEEN: NORTH TO ALASKA

tears filled my eyes, and I told him that Travis was our baby. I expressed my fear that, due to Brian's stage four cancer, I didn't know if this would be our last trip together. There are times when fear overcomes your faith, and your emotions are just too much to handle. A time when it is necessary to express the stuff inside and let it go. I wasn't a sobbing mess, but I was sad, and Don was there to help me process some of this pain. He possessed a quiet comfort, like getting a big hug, and simply his voice and body language immediately drew me to his heart and the compassion he had for me. This cancer stuff is not easy, but there are always people to lean on when you need them.

We formed a special bond and realized that, regardless of our circumstances, we had met each other for a reason. On the ship, we continued to communicate through email. He often checked in on me and Brian to see if there was anything we needed. Later, we scheduled a time to meet for coffee so I would have a chance to see his lovely Carol Anne and he could meet Brian.

We had a wonderful afternoon visit and learned so much more about each other. Carole Anne presented us with the book Don had written. Inside, he had inscribed it with a special message for Travis. Thrilled with such a lovely gesture, we would present it to Travis when we got home.

The rest of the trip went reasonably well. We experienced more than we ever could have imagined.

Whales, dolphins, bald eagles, still blue waters, a calving glacier, sunshine, fresh air, music, and memories. *Thank you, God, for blessing us with this opportunity.* We knew when we got home, we'd hear about the test results, and we prayed the results would be as perfect as our trip to Alaska!

Canada/Alaska border, White Pass Summit, AK 2023

Searching the landscape, Near Ketchikan, AK 2023

THIRTEEN: NORTH TO ALASKA

Great travelling companions, Brother Herve, Brian, Julie and Lisa 2023

Fourteen
Stable is a Big Word

NOT ONE TO complain about his circumstances, Brian helped keep me grounded and positive. One afternoon, after a nap in our Hope room, I woke up angry. It came out of nowhere. "I hate that this is happening to you! I hate seeing what cancer is doing to you." He responds, "There is always a reason." That stuck in my head. It worried me that Brian did not show any anger. How could he process all this stuff and how it was affecting him without feeling angry at someone or something? I talked to God. *What is truly the reason for this? What are we to learn? How are we going to make a difference?*

I'd be lying if I said I wasn't bitter and angry at God. Brian, on the other hand, showed such quiet composure, strength, and resilience. For several years, I had not been going to church. While Mom was in care in Vilna, my Sundays were spent picking up watermelon and heading down Highway 36 to visit her. That became my church practice. I now believe that we do not need a church to practice our faith. It is not a place, but a practice, something that we need to do each and every day. Go to the church of your heart. I ask God to speak to my heart; I pray to do his work and be of service to him. I pray to know him better and to have him work in my life.

When I prayed, Brian said it made him feel calm. Sometimes I didn't want to pray, and when he asked me to, it was difficult to pray. I felt overwhelmed by the magnitude of this disease. I needed to be reminded by Brian that prayer was necessary and comforting. I learned to speak to God as I would a friend. I think this is important. He wants to hear more than all our troubles; he wants to know our joys and be a part of them too. He is more than a comforter; he is our counsellor and confidant. When the attacks kept coming, I reminded Brian that it meant we were close to a breakthrough. Believing in and expecting a miracle took work each and every day, especially when we were going against such a giant. This was our David and Goliath story. A story of faith, courage, and bravery. We continued to believe in God's healing and in Every Perfect Possibility.

We returned to the CCI for results. So far, we had attended thirty-two appointments since January. The miles were exhausting, yet we found a certain tranquility during this time together. We were blessed with this time to share our deepest feelings and connect.

FOURTEEN: STABLE IS A BIG WORD

I know many couples will never experience this in their marriage. Our lives are often consumed by our busyness, and we never seem to have the time—or take the time—for each other. Some of us choose this busyness to avoid dealing with stuff. Life stuff, hard stuff, emotional and messy stuff. We can all fall prey to those avoidance behaviours, when what we truly need is to talk about it and process it. The good, the bad, and the ugly. We all carry some version of this. The shame, guilt, disappointment, grief, resentment, and regret.

While on the road, we listened to music, watched for birds and animals, discussed family, and shared our dreams, potential projects, and possible vacations. Now that I was in the driver's seat for most of our trips, it was a different perspective. Brian had always driven, and often I would be like a cat sleeping in the sunshine. If you put it out into the universe and pay attention, you'll see that it will be reciprocated. God blessed us with so many beautiful moments that I have captured in my mind. Sunrises, sunsets, geese, hawks, eagles, owls, moose, fox, deer, and bear. It was an awakening of the senses. A time of true presence and awareness.

Once again, we sat in a full waiting room. I found out later that many were waiting to be called out for their chemotherapy information sessions. I watched the nurses call their names; some were there alone, while others had a family member or loved one with them. Seeing as Brian's information session was during Covid, we did it virtually, which I thought was so much better. All these faces look troubled and anxious, but at home we were able to sit in comfort and support each other while sipping tea. I guess some things did improve because of the pandemic! If I were to make this choice again, I would definitely suggest staying home to listen virtually. There will be plenty of time spent in hospitals and treatment rooms with other patients. I honestly hope that you will never need to make this choice.

Finally called into the room, they took Brian's weight, and thankfully, he had gained weight! He was complaining now about feeling fat, but honestly, I believed it indicated healing. I was so afraid when he kept losing weight. The nurse got the particulars on how he had been doing. Once again, he mentioned the weakness in his leg. This had been reported since September 2021, but when you have stage four cancer, no one cares about the weakness in your leg. All the puzzling, "non-cancer" stuff was left to our family physician, who was extremely overworked in a rural community with limited resources. Dr. Balash, we appreciate you so much and know that you will always fight for Brian. You have supported us and made the best possible plan for Brian's treatment. We feel very blessed that we were able to get such a dedicated doctor.

The oncologist came in and once again asked if we had checked the reports. Brian responded that he

FOURTEEN: STABLE IS A BIG WORD

had. *I guess he knows?* It was good news. Stable! Finally, all his results showed that he was now stable! *Amen, God is Good!* We had finally found our happy place. No mention of juicy lymph nodes, areas of questionable uptake, or undefined results. We would take this! Finally, *stable*! I sent a text to all our family and friends, informing them of the good news. I truly believed we would not have come this far without all those incredible people, our supporters and prayer teams. I prayed we could continue to provide messages of good news for many years to come.

Fifteen
Testing... Testing...

IN SEPTEMBER 2023, at an appointment with our wonderful doctor in Bonnyville, she continued to probe and assess Brian's leg weakness. We showed her a video of Brian's leg seizure that month; it had occurred after a short period of squats. So much for exercise! Finally, someone was actually listening and agreeing this was a concern. He had been mentioning this leg weakness for two years. It seems whenever you have a cancer diagnosis, everything else becomes less important. This, however, had been the biggest change for us to manage since Brian was diagnosed. The area of the main tumour, the left parietal lobe, just didn't seem the likely cause of his decreased ability to walk.

For many months, we had been talking to the cancer doctors about the weakness in his leg and his tremors, seizures, and loss of mobility. Dr. Balash had been trying her best to order everything possible to help us get to the bottom of this strange but concerning issue.

I still did not believe it was related to the brain, as it was so position-dependent. As we approached home, Brian received a call from our Bonnyville doctor. She had consulted with a neurologist, and felt we needed to get some things figured out. Number one was that they felt the seizures were focal seizures, affecting only a certain part of his body. Although they'd begun as leg seizures, they had progressed to his abdomen and chest. They believed Brian needed to be treated with seizure meds as the issue was likely due to radiation effects and scar tissue. The neurologist wanted to follow up with an urgent brain, CT, and MRI on the lower spine and pelvis. She informed us that they needed to rule out some very serious situations that might be taking place. This was a scary but necessary time—a time to hopefully figure things out or at least eliminate what was not happening. She promised to keep our family doctor in the loop so we could follow up with her.

Back to Edmonton we went for a steroid shot in area L5. The previous MRI showed narrowing of this area and an injection would hopefully help to relieve some of this. Honestly, I was very nervous. I was afraid of this injection. After everything Brian had gone through, this should have been a routine procedure, but my fear was it would somehow make things worse. Completed under ultrasound by a physician, the needle would be inserted beside the spinal cord and would hopefully relieve some pressure. I nervously waited in Brian's little change room and prayed. I didn't want anything else to jeopardize what Brian had left for strength and mobility. He had always said that losing his ability to walk was his biggest fear. Yet he refused to use a cane or anything else because he felt it was giving up. He was a strong and stubborn one, but I was thankful he refused to give up or lose hope. I prayed by faith that, one day, his strength would be restored.

On October 2, 2023, Brian began to have one of his normal leg seizure episodes. It typically never happened at night, so this was a bit more puzzling. Most of these episodes seemed to have been triggered by movement or an awkward position. After a while, we began to feel like this one was going to be different. It didn't appear to be stopping and had moved to his abdomen and chest. An hour and a half into the event, we decided it was time to get to the hospital. We would have to be seen in a small rural hospital during a doctor shortage, and a busy night in the ER could mean terrible delays. To our grave misfortune, we were left waiting on an emergency room bed while other patients were being assessed. The nurse came in to start an IV and then tried Ativan, which should have slowed the seizure activity. It didn't. The seizures continued. They were stronger and were physically exhausting for Brian as we waited for the locum doctor to come in and assess him. These were the most difficult hours we endured during our ordeal with cancer. The unrelenting seizures completely emptied the hope tank.

After a treatment of IV magnesium and seizure meds, Brian was ready to go home at 6:30 a.m. I returned from a short sleep in the parking lot to get him and was saddened by his weakness. I suspected the lengthy seizure activity and the medications had affected his movement, but still I was very afraid he would not walk again. This was the first time I had to use a wheelchair to move him. It was awkward and scary. Many times, I had thought about Brian losing his mobility, but pushing that wheelchair was mentally and emotionally difficult.

When Brian was first diagnosed in 2021, we tackled twenty thousand steps to the Tea House at Lake Louise. This was a treacherous, steady climb, and many parts he could master while I failed miserably. He was always so positive and persistent; he was able to keep me going. Even though he was the one with cancer, he had the spirit and determination to finish. *Push through and succeed*, that was my Brian. He was the one I would always admire, the one who never backed down through all of life's challenges. While others fractured and gave up, he was steadfast in his commitment to complete the task and persevere. Quitting was not an option!

FIFTEEN: TESTING... TESTING...

Climb to Lake Agnes Tea House,
Lake Louise, AB, 2021

Celebrating the climb to 7K feet,
Lake Agnes Tea House, AB, 2021

Adjusting to his limited movement and losing my walking partner was emotionally painful. After cancelling treatment and speeding up the scans, we knew we were in a very unpredictable place. I reached out to several family members and friends and asked for prayers. I refused to let all these negative reports and diagnoses destroy my trust in God. God's Got Ya! It was a "trust without borders" situation. From the beginning of our journey, we had let God lead us to healing, believing in the right doctors and treatments. Maybe we just needed to give it to him. I believed and trusted in God and let him do his work. I felt strongly about this. His divine power had always sheltered me and kept me standing tall in my faith. Sometimes, I was afraid to tell people how this felt. Were they going to think I'd lost my mind? Regardless of the outcome, God had definitely been on this journey with us. I refused to let anyone or anything rob me of believing for and expecting a miracle. I reminded myself to choose my faith over fear. To trust in God and believe that he had us. I believed that God could do the impossible and see us through this dark valley.

> Have I not commanded you? Be strong and of good courage; do not be afraid, nor be dismayed, for the Lord your God is with you wherever you go. (Joshua 1:9, NKJV)

Sixteen
Healed

BY FAR, THIS is the most difficult chapter to write. So much has taken place over the past thirty-six months, and it's hard to believe we've reached this point in time. A time of big faith, big questions, big challenges, and big possibilities! Well, that pretty much sounds like a summary of our last three years. As I begin this chapter of my book, I must admit that I am not sure where to start. This is a time of uncertainty and questioning. Brian is now closing in on his thirty-six- to thirty-nine-month prognosis. He has endured several types of treatments and procedures, each time bouncing back with resilience.

One of the tests I recently encountered was losing a portion of this book. Yes. Gone, missing, and vanished. After almost two months of editing, adding, deleting, and writing a whole chapter, my book vanished. Poof! You must be wondering how this could happen. Well, when I wrote the chapter "God, not

Google," I think I may have given myself a computer curse! I am not tech savvy in any sense of the word, so after a huge panic, I brought my Chromebook to my friend Matt. We believe that, when I started writing my book, I was saving the document on my work drive. I then likely shared the manuscript with myself in my new Google account. I paid no attention to the fact that the actual book was still being stored and saved in its original location on my school drive. When I resigned my position there, my email and all my files were wiped out—including my book! I am so thankful for my amazing friend Brenda who was reviewing and editing it. She had the only existing copy of the book, a PDF version I'd sent to her back in October 2023, nearly three months earlier. At least I didn't lose it all, but it was a tough pill to swallow. Two months of editing and a whole chapter wiped out!

This chapter, "Healed," may just be the end of our cancer journey. We never know what God has in store for us. I tell Brian that maybe there's a reason for losing this part of the book. Maybe God felt I was rushing him, and he wasn't quite ready yet. There is always more that we can learn. I will let God take the lead on this last chapter.

For now, I want to bring you up to speed with everything that's happening and, believe me, that has been a lot! The title of this chapter, like all the others, was chosen before I began writing. That's probably a little unconventional, but it's almost one of those

SIXTEEN: HEALED

guided experiences I have had. We all have those moments, and it's important for us to listen. Whether you call it intuition, instinct, inspiration, or guidance, there is a power from which we all come, and that power is leading us. Listen carefully, and you will receive messages that move you in a certain direction. They may lead you to your purpose. Writing this chapter gives me a feeling of excitement and apprehension. It has been a rough few months. The big "T" word is now front and center in our lives: trust.

Since October, things have been more challenging—let's just say a tad crazy! Cancer is like this, a series of highs and lows. If you are fortunate enough to be afforded time in the battle, you better prepare yourself for this part. It will make you or break you. Cancer changes on a dime. Things look good, you're feeling good, and then wham-o! What just happened? You can quickly enter a whole new set of circumstances and problems. Brian has had sickness, hospitalizations, treatments, urgent scans, new medications, and his first ambulance ride—which he reports you never want to do, as it was pure torture! All he could talk about afterward was, "Why can't they put better suspension on those vehicles?" Honestly, if he could do it, I know he would be the one to modify it or improve it.

Through it all, he has been rock solid and has demonstrated such courage. He has never considered himself to be a victim of cancer. You do not want to give cancer that power over you. He often talks about all the other people who don't make it home from work, who don't have time to tell their children they love them, or to hug and kiss their wives—the ones who are taken from this earth so suddenly. He appreciates the gift of time. The truth is, we never know when our time will come. All our days are numbered, and we live with more gratitude now.

> Do not judge me by my successes, judge me by how many times I fell down and got back up again.[4]

Treatment has been delayed based on the seizures and the need for further testing. A new seizure medication has been added to a full regimen of prescriptions. We joke about Brian having all the drugs you might ever need: our house is filled with pill bottles. The clutter drives me crazy, but hopefully that will soon change. Prior to cancer, he would barely use a Tylenol; now his pill and supplement schedule is recorded daily to make sure he doesn't miss anything.

The doctors had worked to get Brian's scans and brain MRI moved up. We waited to hear from the CCI on changes to the schedule. From the last appointment in Bonnyville, with video evidence of the seizure episodes, we believed it was critical to see what might be happening in the brain to possibly cause these episodes.

MRI day at the CCI was the first day I would use a wheelchair to bring Brian in for testing. It's too far for

SIXTEEN: HEALED

him to safely walk the halls, so he finally agreed to sit while I push. It was a tough sell with someone so stubborn and strong-willed; it felt awkward for both of us. Regardless, we landed where we needed to be, and Brian completed his test.

A few days later at home, we looked at the results of the MRI. The findings indicated *"progression."* I must say it was alarming but not necessarily unexpected. We didn't understand everything in the report, but it was enough to know that we needed some answers. While we waited to hear from our oncologist, I stayed up late one night and decided to email Dr. Siad from Toronto. I felt led to reach out to him for some help at this point in our journey.

Dr. Siad was the first doctor we met via Zoom in November 2021 after Brian's single brain tumour was discovered. He was a neurosurgeon and researcher at a hospital in Toronto and we were fortunate to meet him through our Vancouver team, CTOAM. Initially, he was very interested in removing the tumour, but as we delayed the surgery till after Christmas—and Covid cases shut us all down—the opportunity to remove the tumour was gone. The world was in a pandemic and global healthcare crisis. During our final conversation with him in January 2022, medical care between the provinces was impossible as many hospitals were overwhelmed with Covid patients. This was really a case of you-snooze-you-lose. We decided to wait and spend a nice Christmas with our kids before having the surgery. Well, we lost the chance. In closing, Dr. Siad had always said his patients were like his family, and if we ever needed him, we should reach out.

Within twenty-four hours and the course of a weekend, Dr. Siad sent a response to my email and requested a copy of Brian's last scan results. First thing Monday morning, we were on the phone with the Cross Cancer hospital to arrange for Dr. Siad to have access to the scans. Following his review, he sent this email message:

Dear Lisa and Brian,

Thank you for sending me the link to Brian's recent imaging. I was able to review the recent MRI from October 13.

Two points that are worth making:

1. The appearance of the residual lesion on the recent MRI is much more suggestive of radiation effect than active tumour. We will occasionally use a sequence called MRI perfusion to distinguish between the two. It is sometimes impossible to do so without pathologic confirmation, which can only come from analysis of tumour harvested through surgery.

2. The lesion is in what is called the motor cortex: the part of the brain responsible for right leg and foot movement. In other words, Brian's leg weakness is due to destruction of the part of the brain responsible for that

SIXTEEN: HEALED

> *function by the tumour. Unfortunately, his leg function would not improve with surgery.*
>
> *I am so sorry to give you this news. I hope point #1 offer some relief from the weight of point #2.*
>
> *Sincerely, Dr. Siad*

Thank God, he feels it is not progression but, instead, radiation effect. It was worth celebrating this news—we sent out messages to family, friends, and prayer partners! One step at a time… literally, one step at a time. We would deal with the brain first and then focus on Brian walking again.

As we were still waiting for contact from the CCI, I sent one more email to Dr. Siad asking about his treatment recommendations. He quickly responded with this:

> *Brian should continue on the pembrolizumab—it will be critical to control his systemic cancer.*
>
> *He does not need more radiation for his brain lesions. He might benefit, though, from treatment with a drug called bevacizumab, which can decrease radiation necrosis. It might be something to bring up to his oncologist.*
>
> *Sincerely, Dr. Siad*

We emailed our oncologist with this information and waited for his response about the latest MRI and his treatment plan. Within a few days, Brian received a call from a very apologetic doctor who had not contacted him for nearly three weeks since his urgent MRI. He had already initiated paperwork to build a case for Brian to begin treatment with Bevacizumab as recommended by Dr. Siad and had also sat down with three radiologists to review the recent brain scans. He agreed that it was not active tumour growth but necrosis or dead tissue from radiation treatments. We felt like we'd dodged a bullet! It was such a relief that we weren't dealing with progression here. Although a not-good situation, we accepted this as positive news given the alternative.

In November 2023, Brian was approved and received his first treatment of Bevacizumab, along with his other chemotherapy drug, Pemetrexed. Brian was feeling strong and looking well. We were ready to blast this brain tumour to bits! His first treatment went very well, aside from some rash issues; we didn't notice any significant change in how he was feeling.

I turned to God's Word, this time focusing on the healing within the Bible. There were numerous times in the Bible when Jesus healed. One of the first books I read was called Radical Remission, and within it are several stories of healing. They are truly what has lifted me up from the beginning—the belief that there is always hope, even in the deepest and darkest times of this disease. For anyone faced with this prognosis, I highly recommend reading this book. Every miracle

SIXTEEN: HEALED

within it is a testament of strength, faith, courage, and miracles. It's not a religiously affiliated book, but it is simply story after story of how individuals with a deadly cancer diagnosis made positive changes, listened to divine guidance, and discovered powerful healing. I consider it an uplifting read and each story provided me with ideas about what we could do to improve Brian's chances of having this same experience.

I refused to pick up a book or listen to a podcast without first interpreting how it might help us build our cancer tool kit. There is always a message that is guiding us. Whether in writing, song, or experience, I listened with purpose: a healing purpose. I began to see and believe that this journey was creating something to change the trajectory of our lives and the lives of others. It was coming together, our purpose. God had a hand in taking this diagnosis and helping us turn it around so that others could be a part of growing their faith and believing in our miracle!

During this time, as I had resigned from my job, I had no income. My 2023 income was ten thousand dollars, but even though Brian was on a portion of his income through his disability pension, I never worried. I knew that God would provide for us. I considered us to be retired even though we were far from that time in our lives. Brian loved his job and said he was going to work until he was sixty! I wanted us to feel as though we'd reached this important milestone. It is difficult for two people who love their jobs to just stop and transition to a different time and space. At one point, a helpful lady from employment insurance convinced me that I had to apply for compassionate care benefits. This is a program the government has for individuals who are in palliative care or within six months of death. She assured me that, even if I applied for the program and Brian had a miraculous recovery from his terminal illness, this was perfectly acceptable and within my rights. Somehow, though, it just didn't feel right to me to say that Brian was within six months of his death. When Dr. Balash signed the medical papers, she refused to check the box that said the patient was or could be within six months of death. I never argued or debated this, and the money honestly was not as important as having Brian live and be healthy again. God would help us find a way, and again, we needed to trust him through this experience. To this day, I am happy she never checked that box. What, then, would I have begun to believe? How might this have changed my thoughts, behaviours, or actions?

Boxing Day 2023 started as a normal morning following Christmas and its festivities. Derek was cooking up breakfast for us as he often does when he is home. Brian was tired and slept longer than his usual 6:30 a.m. I saw him moving his left hand and touching it. I knew right away he wasn't feeling well. As I talked to him, I noticed his face. The left side was drooping, and his speech was slurred. Immediately, with the

SIXTEEN: HEALED

eggs Benedict still on the plate, I told Derek, "Get the vehicle—your dad is having a stroke!" This was a bit of breakfast chaos we did not expect! By the time we drove into town, Brian reported that the numbness had disappeared and he was feeling better. His face looked better and, although I still saw a slight droop in his upper lip, he appeared normal again. *Thank God, this is why I pray!*

This began a long process of tests and questioning. Staying positive, I told him this was our Christmas miracle. God was making it all happen; he would make a way for us. Brian received more magnesium and another dreaded ambulance ride to Cold Lake. He was sent home later with no signs of a stroke, nothing remarkable on the CT scan, and a fast-tracked brain MRI. Brian would not have any further signs of this attack, but I insisted he stop taking his TKI, as I always felt that when it built up in his system, he got these bizarre side effects (which I also found documented by the Mayo Clinic).

On December 31, we celebrated a proposal! Scott and Brianna were finally engaged. We'd known for several months about Scott's plans to ask Brianna to marry him, but he had been waiting for the right moment. After a very nervous day chasing down Brianna's dad to ask for her hand in marriage, he finally popped the question. They came over on New Year's Eve to make the announcement, and we toasted the happy couple! I couldn't help but think that this was the start of something amazing. We couldn't have been happier for them! The wedding is to take place in July 2025.

"The Perfect Pair"
Scott and Brianna's engagement, 2023

To celebrate the happy New Year, we set off for the city on January 3. Although Brian's MRI was originally scheduled for the end of January, given the stroke episode, things were happening more quickly. I was feeling confident and tranquil. I was at ease with this test and still feeling that "God's Got Ya" attitude!

SIXTEEN: HEALED

It was my brother Herve's birthday, and I just felt so much happiness and assurance. I fully believed in my heart that we were going to be okay. I was believing for and expecting this miracle. I also felt that God wanted Brian well and that it was time for things to turn around.

On January 4, the big news was that the brain tumour had shrunk to nearly half its original size! Wow, finally we were making progress on this tumour. It had been our nemesis since October 2021, when it was first discovered. The bad actor! It was truly time to say good riddance to this troublemaker. We were on cloud nine and it felt amazing!

Again, we sent out positive messages about Brian's results. The response was an outpouring of love and relief. There is power in prayer, and at times like this when we get to celebrate together, it is so uplifting. I stopped to wonder, *Just what will it feel like to hear that there is no evidence of disease (NED)?* Only God could truly give us this blessing and gift. I remained confident that we would experience this. I told Brian to picture this in his mind and feel the emotions related to healing. To see it, feel it, and experience what it would be like to be told, "Brian you are healed!" While I was meditating on this, I started to cry. It was that powerful!

Later that month, we were tested once again. It was January 22 and this time, it was either a cold, flu, or Covid causing concern about Brian's wellness. I took him to the hospital to be examined as he had developed a deep cough. His magnesium, potassium, and sodium were way off. He was really feeling unwell. Bloodwork and x-rays were ordered. He received IV magnesium and began a course of antibiotics. They prescribed antibiotics for a possible chest infection with no evidence of pneumonia. The x-ray was not completely clear, and we had to wait until the next scan date to ensure that everything was okay in his lungs. Within a week, he began to pick up and, after the Oilers' fourteenth straight win, he was much more positive about the hockey season—and his recovery! It seemed several people were being hit harder this year. Recovery was a slippery slope: one step forward, one backward, and one sideways. They were calling this season the trifecta of illness; Influenza, RSV, and Covid were lurking.

A week later, we were up and off to the city for the rest of Brian's scans—bone and chest/abdomen. Brian was feeling tired and, as always, we both knew it would be a long day. This time, there was no argument about a wheelchair. I parked the truck, and he was already sitting in one, waiting for me to give him his ride down the halls. First, he got his IV and injection for the bone scan. As we moved to another area for his chest CT, he slowly followed the nurse and me down the hallway, then said, "I think I'm having a reaction?" He was feeling strange again and had lost feeling on the left side, arm, and face. He pulled down his mask and, sure enough, the left side of his face was drooping again. The young nurse had him sit while she quickly got additional support. Within a few minutes, he was heading into an unexpected brain CT scan. They were worried about a stroke, but I remained calm. We had seen this before. We told them about all the blood tests and his low magnesium, sodium, and potassium. This might explain why this was happening, but it could also be the Ozzy Brian had taken the evening before. This was the third situation like this since December 26. They always seemed to happen about twelve to fourteen hours after taking Ozzy. Was this when the medication peaked in his system? Had he developed a resistance to it? Was God telling us to stop medicating Brian, or were these possibly strange side effects of the Bevacizumab, which we'd added in November? We would wait to discuss this with the oncologist next week at our routine visit. Brian was cleared once again of any signs of stroke, and the radiologist who reviewed the scans assured us that the brain scan was still looking stable.

February 6, 2024
It seems strange to have reached a point in the book where I'm actually writing in the present tense. I've shared all the background story, and we are here, near the end of part of our journey. Today, we're back at the CCI to see the doctor and try to unravel some of these strange side effects. Brian has already checked

his scans, which we know look good and stable. We discover a new area in the hospital and discuss symptoms with the RN prior to meeting a new intern who comes in to discuss Brian's results and the past three months of treatment. Somehow, their wires have definitely crossed. They've been assuming that Brian's stroke symptoms are on his right side, like his weak leg. We have to stop and correct them. No, the symptoms have always been on the left.

It's all too complicated to understand. It's puzzling; no one can provide a reason or even suggest something that may be causing these symptoms. The intern discusses the case with our doctor, and they both come into the room. He launches the conversation by reviewing how the medication has been working, and the positive results on the scans—but quickly changes direction with some difficult and deflating messages. "It may be time to choose quality of life over quantity of life." He goes on to credit us for being so active in Brian's treatment and says Brian's case has taken him into uncharted territory. He actually tells us he is "flying by the seat of his pants!" Later, Brian says, "How can I have faith and trust in my doctor when he tells me this?" I understand there's no way to explain all the things happening to Brian during his course of treatment. He puts the ball in our court and asks us, "What do you want to do? Do we continue treating you or is it time to stop treatment?" Positive results that come with a heavy blow!

SIXTEEN: HEALED

We refuse to tell our family and friends this part of our conversation. Keeping it positive is very important to us. Many times, we've filtered the information we receive and just given the good stuff. Before we leave the hospital room, I see Brian with his shoulders dropped and I can feel his sadness. I stand in front of him and say, "Quit it. We're not letting anyone steal our joy and our faith." Whose report will I choose to listen to? Who really knows our days and the plan for our lives? God. I will not let Brian leave this hospital without trying to turn things around.

Again, we send a positive text to our family and friends about the scan results. We fail to provide details of the gloomy conversations and continue to focus on prayer and healing. The most difficult thing is waiting for God to lead us. I search his Word and wait to hear him. You may think it's bizarre, but this whole experience has been led by the Creator. As difficult as it is to finish a story that's in transition, I believe God wants this part of our life to be told. We have reached a point in time where this story or this book will end. I am confident that our next story will be filled with blessings.

February 12, 2024
Today I spent the morning with students at the high school. It is our candygram and carnation Valentine's sale for the Interact club. It still brings me so much joy to spend time with our youth and make a difference in

the lives of others. Like our hope campaign, this little project makes me feel like we are spreading joy and happiness in a world that certainly needs as much love as we can give it.

> You cannot do a kindness too soon, for you never know how soon it will be too late.[5]

My message is to plant these seeds daily, to plant seeds of hope, love, and peace. Nurture those seeds. Give energy to these things and not to all the other negative or material things society wants us to focus on. Don't get caught up in the weeds. No matter how big the world may seem, we are all connected, and we truly need to bring more light into it. Despite your circumstances, you can always choose kindness.

The title of this book, *Every Perfect Possibility*, came to me in a dream. A loud voice woke me from my sleep and said those three words. Like many other dream messages, I knew this was a book that needed to be written. The title represents so much to me as it became the way that we would approach this challenge and Brian's cancer diagnosis: with a belief in *Every Perfect Possibility*. An unshakeable possibility consciousness would hold us and strengthen us. Of course, this also meant surrendering to God, following his lead, having faith in his plan, and offering a trust without borders.

SIXTEEN: HEALED

> With man this is impossible, but with God all things are possible. (Matthew 19:26, NIV)

February 16, 2024
Today is Brian's three-year cancer-versary! Wow, it's hard to believe that we've spent the last three years of our life in this battle. When I look back at our pictures, I see all the changes and I remember all the moments: the sad, the happy, the scary, the anxious, the joyous, the troubled, and the blessed. Our adversity roller coaster has taken us on quite a ride of emotions. I am confident that this ride would never have been the same experience or brought us the same results without the guidance and love of God.

I created this post for our Facebook page, and I appreciated reading how much our journey has impacted others:

> *He was 49 years old when he received a stage four cancer diagnosis. Today marks his third year cancer-versary! A difficult day but one filled with gratitude that we have made it this far. I could not be more proud of this man, our family, our friends, and our community. Thank you for your support and prayers, for lending us hope when we were feeling down, for your calls, texts, and hugs at just the right time. For God and our faith.*

> *Today marks a day of sweet but quiet celebration. To embrace the unknown as powerful and full of possibilities. Today and every day we celebrate life; live it, nurture it, and embrace it. Each day, every day, truly show up for your life. Our days are all numbered but within alignment with the divine plan. Today and every day place your trust in "Every Perfect Possibility." Know it. Live it!*
>
> *We will publish our story, our journey, in the next few months, and I hope and pray that you will welcome our words into your hearts.*
>
> *Thank you for your continued prayers and positive energy. #POWER in prayer!*

I believe that we all have a purpose and some way we can impact the world. I believe that our story has changed lives and will continue to change lives. It has most certainly changed us. It has strengthened our family and brought about a new perspective. God has delivered a message to and through us. In turn, I pray our story leads you to strengthen your faith and to connect with the Creator. Live in the moment and be present. Whether those moments are filled with quiet nature or chaos, appreciate it. Find the *aha* in each and every day. Big or little, look for it and soak it in. Ask yourself, What was my *aha* moment today?

As we begin Holy Week, before Easter—Jesus' death and resurrection—I am reminded of what God

SIXTEEN: HEALED

has done for me. I am reminded of my blessings. God loves me regardless of my faults. His son Jesus died for our sins, to offer us forgiveness, eternal life, and healing. Even in the times we have wavered, he loves us. His power is undeniable. I choose to live life with gratitude and be more present. As the beauty of spring brings forth new life, hope, and possibilities, surrender to this experience. Let your faith draw you out of your troubled mind. Trust the process and wake up to living life.

I hate to leave everyone hanging. I can't give you the full ending or deliver a grand finale. But that hasn't been my goal with this book. My goal has been to tell our story, never to finish it. There is so much more to come and only he knows what it will be. I can assure you that I'm not giving up on God. I will remain hopeful and believe in his miracle power. Love speaks a language that is far beyond time, space, or species, and there exists a power that is so vast it can connect us with the divine.

I now set the intention and affirm that our next story will be one of peace, praise, and blessing. Life is providing us with everything we need to bring forth the best of who we truly are. Faith is the willingness to accept what is and to know that you did the best you could. It is believing in what you cannot see. I encourage you to embrace the unknown as powerful and full of possibilities. When we are living our best lives, we can trust that God is guiding us.

Together, we found God.

Count it all joy, my brothers, when you meet trials of various kinds, for you know that the testing of your faith produces steadfastness. And let steadfastness have its full effect, that you may be perfect and complete, lacking in nothing. (James 1: 2-4, ESV)

Footprints in the Sand

One night I dreamed a dream.
As I was walking along the beach with my Lord,
Across the dark sky flashed scenes from my life.
For each scene, I noticed two sets of footprints
in the sand,
One belonging to me and one to my Lord.
After the last scene of my life flashed before me,
I looked back at the footprints in the sand.
I noticed that at many times along the path of my life,
Especially at the very lowest and saddest times,
There was only one set of footprints.
This really troubled me, so I asked the Lord about it.
"Lord, you said once I decided to follow you,
You'd walk with me all the way.
But I noticed that during the saddest and most troublesome times of my life,
There was only one set of footprints.
I don't understand why, when I needed you the most,
you would leave me."

SIXTEEN: HEALED

*He whispered, "My precious child, I love you and will
never leave you
Never, ever, during your trials and testings.
When you saw only one set of footprints,
It was then that I carried you."[6]*

About the Author

LISA DRIBNENKI (MICHAUD) was raised in the small farming community of St. Lina, Alberta. She attended school in Mallaig, Alberta. In 1989 she moved to Lac La Biche, where she met her husband, Brian, while pursuing her postsecondary education. They have been married for thirty years and have three sons: Derek, Scott, and Travis.

For over twenty years, Lisa worked as a social worker for the government of Alberta in Children's Services and Income and Employment Support. She ended her career in human services as a guidance counsellor at J.A. Williams High School in Lac La Biche. To this day, she is a strong advocate for youth leadership and community development.

Lisa and Brian still reside in Lac La Biche. Lisa continues to lead youth within the Rotary Interact Club, believing in the power of "Service Above Self" to make a difference locally and abroad. Faith is courageous living, and Brian and Lisa choose to live with a strong faith in God and a *possibility consciousness.*

Cruising the Konningsdam, Alaska, 2023

Further Reading

Borysenko, Joan, and Miroslav Borysenko. *The Power of the Mind to Heal: Renewing Body, Mind, and Spirit.* Carlsbad, CA: Hay House, 1994.

Chopra, Deepak. *Quantum Healing: Exploring the Frontiers of Mind/Body Medicine.* New York, NY: Bantam, 1990.

Coenn, Daniel. *Mark Twain: His Words.* Munich, Germany: Book Rix, 2014. Kindle Edition.

Coonan, Dianne M. *The Lies I Once Believed, the Truth I Now Live.* Winnipeg, MB: Word Alive Press, 2019.

Hay, Louise L. *Meditations to Heal Your Life.* Carlsbad, CA: Hay House, 2002.

Jampolsky, Gerald G., MD. *Love Is Letting Go of Fear.* New York, NY: Random House, 2011.

Lipton, Bruce H. *The Biology of Belief: Unleashing the Power of Consciousness, Matter, and Miracles*. Carlsbad, CA: Hay House, 2007.

Mandela, Nelson. *Long Walk to Freedom: The Autobiography of Nelson Mandela*. New York: Back Bay Books, 1995.

Powers, Margaret Fishback. "Footprints." In *Footprints: The True Story Behind the Poem,* Revised Edition. New York: Harper Collins, 2012.

Teel, Roger. *This Life is Joy: Discovering the Spiritual Laws to Live More Powerfully, Lovingly, and Happily*. New York, NY: Penguin Random House, 2014.

Turner, Kelly A. *Radical Remission: Surviving Cancer Against All Odds*. Broadway, NY: Harper Collins, 2015.

Wommack, Andrew. *God Wants You Well: What the Bible Says About Walking in Divine Health*. Colorado Springs, CO: Harrison House, 2010.

Endnotes

1 Daniel Coenn, *Mark Twain: His Words* (Munich, Germany: Book Rix, 2014), Kindle Edition.

2 Bruce H. Lipton, *The Biology of Belief: Unleashing the Power of Consciousness, Matter, and Miracles* (Carlsbad, CA: Hay House, 2009), 116.

3 "Chief Dan George Quotes," *That One Rule*, Accessed August 12, 2024, https://thatonerule.com/rule/chief-dan-george-quotes.

4 Nelson Mandela, *Long Walk to Freedom*: *The Autobiography of Nelson Mandela* (New York: Back Bay Books, 1995).

5 "Ralph Waldo Emerson Quotes," *Brainy Quote,* Accessed August 12, 2024, https://www.brainyquote.com/quotes/ralph_waldo_emerson_106295.

6 Margaret Fishback Powers, "Footprints," (1964).